What Can I Do with My Herbs?

NUMBER FORTY

W. L. Moody Jr. Natural History Series

What Can I Do

TEXAS A&M UNIVERSITY PRESS   COLLEGE STATION

with My Herbs?

How to Grow,
Use & Enjoy
These Versatile Plants

BY JUDY BARRETT

Art by Victor Z. Martin

LIBRARY OF CONGRESS
CATALOGING-IN-PUBLICATION DATA

Barrett, Judy, 1945–
    What can I do with my herbs? : how to grow,
use, and enjoy these versatile plants / by Judy Barrett ;
art by Victor Z. Martin.
        p. cm. — (W. L. Moody Jr. natural history series ; no. 40)
Includes index.
    ISBN-13: 978-1-60344-092-9 (printed case (cloth) : alk. paper)
    ISBN-10: 1-60344-092-5 (printed case (cloth) : alk. paper)
    1. Herbs—Handbooks, manuals, etc.   2. Herb gardening—
Handbooks, manuals, etc.   3. Cookery (Herbs)—Handbooks,
manuals, etc.   I. Title.   II. Series.
SB351.H5B323   2009
635'.7—dc22
                                                2008031016

Contents

What Can I Do with My Herbs?

What Can I Do with My Herbs?

A certain mystery surrounds herbs. What *are* herbs anyway? I like the definition offered by the United States National Arboretum in Washington, D.C.: "An herb is any plant that serves a purpose other than providing food, wood, or beauty." In other words, herbs are useful plants, not just ornamental or mundane. They have a lot of different forms, looks, smells, and tastes, but the one thing they have in common is their ability to serve at least one purpose, and most often more than one.

Because of the diversity and mysterious nature of herbs, many people are a little bit afraid of them. And, for some bizarre reason, we are more afraid of fresh herbs than we are of those little jars of dried stuff at the grocery store. But, we need not be afraid. Herbs are our friends!

Many misconceptions are associated with herbs. Some people believe they only grow in tiny pots on the windowsill. Others believe they are difficult to grow and even more difficult to use. Then, there is the belief that if you have herbs, you have to be doing something with them all the time. Nothing could be further from the truth.

Many herbs are large plants that grow beautifully in the landscape. Those little windowsill pots are almost always too small for a plant to grow happily in, and most windows do not provide enough sunlight. The herbs listed in this book will grow throughout most of the United States if given the right conditions. Those limited to specific climate zones are noted. Herbs are easy to grow, and many grow like the proverbial weed. In fact, some *are* the proverbial weed!

And finally, herbs do not come with any obligation. You can do things with them—cook, craft, comfort—or you can just look out the window at them and enjoy the view. Herbs are the easiest plants in the world to enjoy.

In the garden, herbs perform a wide range of jobs. They can attract beneficial insects, repel pests, encourage growth of other plants, and, at the same time, be lovely or tasty or fragrant in and of themselves.

I recommend that you grow your herbs without chemicals. Naturally grown herbs make perfect sense. Most herbs are pest-free anyway, and many can be made into natural pest repellants that will serve nicely without endangering you, your family, or your pets.

Once you begin growing herbs or noticing them at the grocery store, you may start looking for new ways to use them. There are plenty of choices. Gardeners have been cultivating and gathering herbs for as long as records have been kept. Ancients gathered herbs for medicines, magic, and to freshen their homes. Various strewing herbs were popular in places where housecleaning was an unknown art. Those same herbs that were once thrown on the floor to temper bad smells are now used to make wonderful potpourris and wreaths—so our homes can smell better and look nice, too!

Potpourri is a mixture of dried flower petals, herbs, and other plant materials blended with spices and oil for fragrance. Making potpourri from dried materials is easy. You can mix and match colors, textures, and scents, depending on what you like and what is available in your garden. You can find recipes in most craft books. Adding essential oils helps the fragrance last longer and allows you to design just the scent you want.

Wreaths can be made of most herbs—either dried or fresh. Culinary herbs can be fashioned into herbal wreaths that can then be used in the kitchen. Herbal wreaths smell good and look wonderful year-round. You can also make dried arrangements of herbs to freshen a room. The Victorian tussy-mussie, a nosegay of dried flowers, is making a comeback, and many herb-lovers make these little bouquets as gifts and decorative items.

Bath and personal products can be made from homegrown herbs—and as a bonus, when you make it yourself, you know what you are putting on your body. Look at the labels of some of the products you use now, and you might want to switch for a while to something you can identify! Herbs can make your bath a relaxing, therapeutic experience; they can rinse your hair clean and give it a healthy shine; they can soften your skin and help control dandruff. Many herbs are said to have a good effect on your hair. While rosemary can make dark hair more lovely, calendula has been used to brighten light hair. Lavender is said to stimulate hair growth. If you like the scent of an herb, you may want to rinse your hair with it by making a decoction and pouring it over your hair. Leave it on for 20 minutes, then rinse. Knowledgeably exploring the ways herbs can make you look and feel better is an enjoyable way to use your herbs.

Herbs also have been known and used for thousands of years for medicinal purposes. The monks who grew their physic gardens on the monastery grounds were charged with the health of the community, and they knew the beneficial properties of herbs. While herbs will not take the place of modern medicine, more and more doctors are becoming aware of the usefulness of herbs as gentle treatments. Learning about medicinal uses of herbs is enlightening.

CAUTION: Herbs are often powerful plants and should not be used or taken as medicine without the advice of a professional. This book does not prescribe or recommend medicinal treatments; I just report and describe traditional uses. If you want to be treated with herbal medicines, contact someone who really knows how they work and how best to use them.

Herbs are often used fresh or dried. In addition, there are some specific forms of preparation that you will find mentioned in books about herbs. Here is a quick definition of those terms:

Infusion: This is essentially the same as tea. Pour boiling water over the herb (root, bark, leaves, flowers, or whatever) and let steep for a while. Strain and use. Although many people think of tea as something you drink, an infusion can also be used in a variety of other ways—sprays, rinses, and more.

Decoction: This is made by pouring cold water over the herb. The mixture is then brought to a boil. Let it simmer for 20–30 minutes, then cool and strain out the plant material.

Tincture: This is a preparation made by combining herbs with alcohol. Vodka is the most commonly used spirit since it has little taste of its own, but some people use wine or other spirits.

Poultice: This is used externally for hurts, bruises, and other wounds and sores. Generally, the herb is crushed or chopped and sometimes mixed with water to make a paste. It can be put directly on the affected part and then covered with a bandage or put into a cloth such as cheesecloth and wrapped over the hurt. Poultices are old-fashioned ways to treat hurts and wounds, but they are often still effective. Warming the herbal mix can add to the soothing effect.

Extract: This preparation is best achieved by experts. I do not include the use of essential oils in this book because that extraction is not something that most amateurs can accomplish. You can buy essential oils and experiment with them, but that is not really within the realm of growing and enjoying herbs.

Herb teas are used both as refreshment and as palliatives, depending on the blend. One of the most common teas, peppermint, is said to help with indigestion, gas, nausea, menstrual cramps, colds, and flu, yet it is also a delicious tea to enjoy with a friend. You can make herb tea with either fresh or dried leaves. In the summer, I simply add mint leaves to water and ice to make a quick, refreshing drink. By drying some of your herb leaves, you can enjoy tea year-round. Here are a few herbs that make good tea—mix and match to suit your taste—anise, anise hyssop, basil, bergamot, catnip, chamomile, scented geranium, lemon balm, lemon verbena, all mints, rosemary, and thyme.

Of course, the most widely recognized use of herbs is in food. They add interest and flavor to all kinds of dishes. Herbs can be used to replace salt by adding flavor to food. This is great if you are trying to reduce the amount of salt in your diet. Herbs can turn a bland dish into something special, but remember that more is not always better when it comes to herbs. Many of these plants have concentrated flavor and can overpower your dish instead of enhancing it if you use too much. When you are experimenting, always begin with a little bit and work up from there. On the other hand, if you are using a recipe, use two to three times as much fresh herb as the recipe calls for dried. Fresh herbs are full of water, so the volume is increased accordingly.

Most culinary herbs make delicious vinegars. These are good to use in salad dressings or as dressings all by themselves for salads, steamed vegetables, coleslaw, cooked greens, or whatever else you generally put vinegar on. They also make wonderful gifts. Simply fill a quart jar with herb leaves that have been smashed to release their flavor, cover with vinegar, and let it sit for a week or two. Strain out the herbs and pour the liquid into a decorative bottle. You can add a couple of stems of herbs to the vinegar to make it look good. Some herbal vinegars are prettier than others. Purple basil makes a lovely rosy-colored vinegar, and chive blossom vinegar will result in a pale pink brew. Herb combinations also make good vinegars. If the herbs go well together in other dishes, they will go well in vinegar. For example, basil, oregano, and garlic are good together in vinegar, just as they are in spaghetti sauce.

You can also make herb butters out of many culinary herbs. These butters are useful in dressing potatoes, steamed vegetables, pasta, fish, steak, or other dishes. Simply chop up your herb or herbs and blend well with softened butter. You can make small balls of your favorites and put them in the freezer. Then you will have them ready to toss into a dish any time. You can freeze herbs in oil in the same way. Be careful with herb oils, though, because they can become rancid or worse in short order. Be sure to keep the oil refrigerated, and freeze it if you want to keep it more than a couple of days.

You can mix your favorite herb flavors into dried combinations and give them as gifts or put them in shaker jars to use in your own kitchen. Remember, dried herbs lose their flavor quickly, especially if exposed to heat or light, so put them in containers that protect them from light and store them in a cool place.

Once you pick your herbs or bring them home from the store, you can keep them fresh in a couple of ways. Cilantro, parsley, mint, and other herbs with soft leaves should be stored in a bouquet in a glass of water in the refrigerator. Cover the tops loosely with plastic wrap so that some air gets in and circulates around the leaves. Woodier herbs like sage, rosemary, and thyme should be placed in a perforated bag or wrapped in plastic wrap and stored in the refrigerator's crisper.

REMEMBER: Not all herbs are edible. Learn about your herbs before you start tossing them into the stew pot.

Herbs also make wonderful cut bouquets. You can use them alone or add them to other fresh flowers from the garden. Rosemary and tansy are great background greenery to set off colorful flowers. Bergamot, Mexican mint marigold, calendula, and other flowering herbs make great bouquets all by themselves. Herbs brighten and freshen the house like no other plants.

Enjoy them!

Víctor Z. Martin
2007

Artemisia Artemisia spp.

⁕ *Learn about it.* Artemisias are wonderfully fragrant plants. Some are more pleasantly fragrant than others, but all have a strong scent that adds to their usefulness. They all have finely cut leaves, and some grow very large. Most have toxic properties. Many are gray, and some are bright green. This large family of plants was named for Artemisia, Queen of Persia and Greece in 353 B.C. She was also a famous botanist and medical researcher and learned about the medicinal uses of many herbal plants, including the two hundred or so in this genus named after her. If you don't like that story, others say the genus is named for Artemis (Diana), goddess of the hunt. That is one of the great things about herbal lore—stories abound, and all are fun to hear.

Common wormwood (*Artemisia absinthium*) is poisonous when taken in excess. There are stories of French painters sitting around drinking absinthe and going mad. Rumor has it that van Gogh would have refrained from slicing off one of his ears if he had not been indulging in absinthe quite so often. Wormwood was used to make this powerful drink, and absinthe production has since been outlawed, but Roman wormwood is still a component in Vermouth and Campari.

In the seventeenth century, wisdom said that mixing wormwood with oil and rubbing it on your head would prevent or cure baldness. The herb was also used by young men to encourage their beards to grow.

Although people should not try to dose themselves with wormwood or any other herb without consulting an expert, there is growing evidence that chemicals in certain artemisias, and particularly sweet annie (*A. annua*), are good for treating malaria. TechnoServe (Technology in the Service of Mankind, a nonprofit organization) assists African farmers in growing sweet annie as a cash crop, which benefits the farmers and malaria sufferers as well. Ongoing research into the medicinal properties of this group of plants is encouraging and has shown that they may also be selectively toxic to breast cancer, prostate cancer, and leukemia cells.

✻   *Grow it.* There are several types of artemisia that are fun to grow. Wormwood is the largest group and most widely grown of this herb family. A bitter tasting herb, wormwood has several popular names and is available in many varieties. Wild wormwoods such as estafiate (*A.* spp.), which is native to the Southwest and Mexico, have been grown and used for centuries in hot, dry areas. Silver king and silver queen (*A. albula*), silver mound (*A. schmidtiana*), beach wormwood, old woman, and dusty miller (*A. stellerana*), Roman wormwood (*A. pontica*), and Powis Castle (*A. arborescens* × *absinthium*) all make silver-leaved, mounding, shrubby plants that are great background material in your garden. Powis Castle is the most mannerly of the silver-leaved plants and the least likely to grow out of control and become a weed. Green varieties such as southernwood (*A. abrotanum*), mugwort (*A. vulgaris*), and sweet annie (*A. annua*) are also beautiful plants and have different scents. Powis castle is said to attract ladybugs, always a good thing. Sweet annie is the only annual in this group. The rest of the plants are perennial and most are evergreen in temperate climate gardens. Sweet annie reseeds freely if left to go to seed.

All are excellent garden plants that serve as good back-of-the-bed plants to set off brightly colored flowers in the foreground. Don't plant your artemisia near anise, beans, caraway, fennel, peas, sage, dill, or coriander, though. In other words, it is probably not a good idea to plant wormwood in the food garden. All artemisia like full sun and good drainage, but they are not particular about soil and almost never need fertilizing. To keep them from getting too big, cut them back in the spring before growth starts. You can cut them back by half without worrying about damaging the plants. They are drought-tolerant, pest-free, and easy-to-grow plants that will be happy in almost any garden.

Take cuttings for new plants in March or October. Almost all perennial artemisias are easily propagated from cuttings but are difficult to grow from seed.

The exception to all of the above is tarragon (*A. dracunculus* var. *sativa*). Tarragon is an herb valued by gourmets and one of the only artemisias that is well suited for consumption. The only edible artemisia, it is also much more picky about where it grows. It is available in both French and Russian types, but the Russian has little flavor, so stick to French if you want to cook with it. Tarragon loves cool weather and is very hard to grow in the South and Southwest United States. Both heat and humidity make the plant collapse. If you can grow it, give it good, rich soil and bright light with good drainage.

✦ *Don't eat it.* Except for tarragon, artemisias are not to be taken internally. Although they have been used for centuries as medicinal herbs, home remedies that involve toxic plant material are just too risky for amateurs to try. Wormwood got its name from its ability to kill internal worms, but the active chemicals vary widely within the genus and from plant to plant.

✦ *Deter with it.* Because they contain toxic elements, artemisias can be great pest repellants. One common name is *garderobe* (French for "clothing protector") because they repel moths and other damaging insects. You can help repel pests both indoors and outdoors with artemisia concoctions.

Bug Bags: Mix 2 tablespoons dried southernwood or other artemisia with 2 tablespoons dried lavender and 2 tablespoons dried mint. Sew mix into small sachets. Put in drawers, chests, and closets to repel insects in clothing and linens.

Bug Spray: Make a decoction of 8 ounces wormwood leaves simmered in 4 pints water for 30 minutes. Stir, strain, and let cool. Add 1 teaspoon castile soap and spray on the leaves of ornamental plants afflicted with insect pests. Do not spray on food or food plants. This spray may repel or kill aphids, flea beetles, moths, snails, slugs, fleas, and may even run off snakes. Spray around the edges of your ornamental borders to keep pests away.

A border backed with artemisia next to the house will help keep pests away. It is also said to repel animals that come looking for a way into the house. Hanging bunches of artemisia near the doorway will repel flies and other unwelcome critters, including, according to lore, evil spirits and goblins. Leaves sprinkled on the ground where your pets commonly lie are good to repel fleas. You can use them inside as well on the pet's bed. Licking a few leaves will not hurt animals.

✸ *Dry it.* Because the scent of artemisias is long-lasting, they make great dried arrangements and wreath bases. Even after the plant has dried, the characteristic scent remains. Sweet annie is particularly nice for herbal bases because it has a fresh, pleasant smell that combines well with other scents. Stuff it into a metal wreath base or affix it to a straw wreath form, then add other elements to create beautiful decorations for any season. You can even use the same base and change the ornaments as the seasons change. You can use the artemisia as soon as you cut it and let it dry naturally on the wreath. You can also hang artemisias to air dry in bunches and use them in dried arrangements, bouquets and potpourri. Make sure you select a variety with a scent you like.

✸ *Freshen with it.* The sweet smell of artemisias is a natural air freshener. Bunches of the branches hung throughout the house will give it a nice, clean, gentle scent that will persist for a long time. Women used to carry bouquets of artemisia and mint to keep themselves fresh and alert during long sermons or journeys. A similar bouquet was used in courts to protect from gaol (jail) fever. Whenever something is unpleasantly smelly, a nice fresh scent helps, and artemisias offer a wide range of fresh scents.

Victor Z. Martin
2007

Basil *Ocimum basilicum*

✺ *Learn about it.* Basil is one of the most popular herbs around and has been for centuries. A native of Africa and Asia, it has been treasured since ancient times. Legend has it that basil was found growing around Jesus' tomb after the resurrection. It was used in Greek Orthodox churches in the preparation of Holy Water. In India, one of its native lands, it was highly prized and was used by Indians on which to swear their oath in court. In Haiti, it is believed to offer a powerful protection from evil spells, and in Mexico, it is sometimes carried in a pocket to attract money.

✺ *Grow it.* There are lots of different varieties of basil. The most common is sweet basil, which is green and has the classic basil flavor. Other varieties include cinnamon, lemon, ruffles, purple ruffles, spicy globe, Greek, purple, lettuce leaf, sacred, Thai, Mexican spice, and more. One source lists more than 150 varieties. Because it is so popular, new varieties are discovered and developed on a fast track. Basil is easy to grow in a sunny garden. It demands sun and warm weather and will quickly succumb at the first hint of frost. You can plant basil from seeds or from transplants. Some say that plants from seed bolt less quickly. In either case, you may want to plant a new crop every few weeks because the leaves lose their good flavor when the plant flowers and goes to seed. Keep pinching off the flowers as long as you can to maintain flavor, but after a while the plant will flower no matter what you do. Then just enjoy the flowers, which are pretty and attractive to beneficial insects. Give basil plants plenty of moisture.

Basil is a good companion plant to tomatoes, asparagus, and most vegetables. They like the same conditions and seem to encourage each other's growth. Tomatoes and basil are also very tasty served together. You can set both plants in the garden at the same time since they are both sensitive to cold. Don't plant basil near rue, cabbage, or snap beans. They seem to discourage each other's growth.

Basil is an annual, but many varieties reseed year after year. Purple ruffle seems especially good at returning every spring. You can also save the seeds of your favorite variety and plant them again next spring. To plant seed, place on top of soil and sprinkle just a little sand or sifted soil on top. Don't bury the seeds. Keep the seed bed watered and watch them grow. Pinch your plants often to keep new leaves forming and to make the plants bushy. Eat the leaves you pinch off, of course. Pinching also discourages flower production.

✭   *Eat it.* This is the true goal of all basil gardening. Nothing is better than sliced homegrown tomatoes sprinkled with fresh basil. The addition of salt, pepper, mozzarella cheese, onion, olive oil, vinegar, or other things is just icing on the cake. Basil's flavor is in its scent, so if you are cooking with it, add it at the last minute to retain the essential oils and smell.

Basil is best known as a companion to tomatoes—spaghetti sauce, fresh or cooked, sliced tomatoes, pizza. Anything that combines the two is delightful, and chefs around the world have made their names on these variations. The other famed use of basil is in pesto. This smashed up combination is great on hot pasta, cold pasta, vegetables, baked potatoes, toasted crusty bread, crackers, and eaten from a spoon when nobody is looking.

Pesto: You can make pesto in a mortar and pestle or in a food processor. Purists have their rules, but it tastes just great either way. Gather 2 cups fresh basil leaves, ½ cup Parmesan cheese, ½ cup olive oil, ⅓ cup pine nuts, 3 garlic cloves. Salt to taste. Combine basil and nuts, add garlic and salt, add cheese, and finally, slowly add oil until completely mixed. If you want to freeze your pesto, leave out the cheese and add it after the mixture has thawed and you are ready to use it. Pesto is easy to freeze, and that is one of the best ways to preserve the flavor of basil since the leaves themselves turn black and yucky when they are frozen and lose their flavor when dried. Pesto is definitely a flexible recipe that should be made to your taste. You can increase or decrease the amounts of any of the ingredients, substitute walnuts, pecans, or other nuts for pine nuts, swap Romano cheese for Parmesan, and add pepper or whatever other flavors you like.

★ *Attract with it.* Beneficial insects love the flowers of basil plants.

★ *Deter with it.* Basil plants repel flies and mosquitoes and may be helpful in deterring thrips on plants growing nearby. If you are in the garden and the mosquitoes start biting, tear off a leaf of basil, crush it and rub it on your skin to help keep those nasty little critters away. Pots or hanging baskets of basil near a sunny door will discourage flying insects from coming in the house.

★ *Bathe with it.* A fresh infusion added to the bath water creates an invigorating bath that will get you ready for a night on the town or a day at work.

★ *Soothe with it.* A tea of basil leaves is said to aid digestion, soothing the stomach after a heavy meal. A few leaves steeped in wine is said to create a general tonic for feeling better all over.

Bay Laurel *Laurus nobilis*

❉   *Learn about it.* Bay, sweet bay, and bay laurel are among the common names of this ancient plant. It has been around since prehistoric days and has been revered in many cultures. The Oracle at Delphi ate a bay leaf before expounding her wisdom. The tree was sacred to Apollo, the god of prophesy, so the Oracle apparently knew where to get her information. The roof of the Temple at Delphi was made of bay leaves. The common use of bay in Greek and Roman architecture has resulted in the adaptation of the leaves into a standard architectural element. For example, the tops of columns, pediments, borders, and other standard features of buildings often are shaped like the bay leaf. The bay laurel wreath is a mark of excellence. Wreathes of bay were used to crown poets and athletes, and recently that practice has been reinstituted at the Olympic Games.

There are several other plants generally known as bay—Canary Island bay, gold bay, California bay, and willow leaf bay. The California bay (*Umbellulari californica*) is also called Oregon myrtle, California laurel, pepperwood, headache tree (because it causes them), and sometimes—adding to the confusion—bay laurel. This should not be confused with the bay laurel also called sweet bay.

CAUTION: While bay laurel (*Laurus nobilis*) is a favorite in the kitchen, many of these other plants that have "bay" in the name are said to be poisonous and should not be used except for ornamental purposes.

✹   *Grow it.* Bay laurel can be grown in many forms—large shrub, small tree, topiary standard, container grown plant. Most people start their plant in a container because it is slow-growing and takes a while before it is big enough to go into the landscape. If you buy a large plant, expect it to take a season or two to get its roots well established so it can start growing on top. Once it is established, it will grow steadily and can reach 40 feet or more in climates where it is really happy. Bay cannot tolerate exceptionally cold winters. It is hardy outdoors in Zones 7–10. In other areas, it can be grown in containers and taken inside in the winter.

Bay is evergreen and, as such, is a good plant to serve as structure in your garden. It can mix well into herbaceous borders or stand alone as a specimen plant. It can anchor a foundation planting or sit grandly in a container on the patio or deck.

Bay likes moisture-retentive, well-drained, fertile soil. It can take full sun or part shade and will grow as an understory tree with large deciduous trees. Even though your transplant may be small, give it a good sized container to grow in so you don't have to transplant it often. If you want to grow it as a standard, start pruning to shape as soon as it is tall enough. If you are growing it in a container, make sure the plant has sufficient water. Bay likes soil on the moist side, but in the ground, it quickly becomes drought-tolerant when it is well established. A good all-purpose organic fertilizer that contains trace minerals, when applied a couple of times a year, should keep the plant healthy and growing well. Mulching around the base of the tree will keep moisture levels even and prevent weed growth.

✹   *Cook with it.* There is a myth abroad that bay leaves can only be used dried. That simply is not true. Like any other herb, fresh is better every time. The flavor is brighter and more intense in a fresh leaf than in a dried one. Unlike many fresh herbs, bay leaves keep their flavor even during long cooking, so they are good for soups, stews, and other simmered dishes. They are well suited to cooking with all types of dried beans, and bay leaf is an important ingredient in corned beef.

Unlike most plants, bay leaves do not soften with cooking, so after your dish is done, remove the bay leaf and add it to the compost heap. You can chop bay leaves up very fine and add to cheese and butters, but generally the leaves are sharp, pointed, and not pleasant to eat. Their best use is for flavoring.

In England there is a tradition of using bay leaves to flavor custard and rice puddings. Bay adds a subtle, spicy taste. To make a bay-flavored custard, infuse the milk with about 12 fresh bay leaves, then follow your regular recipe. To infuse the milk, bring it to a boil. Remove immediately from heat and add the crumbled leaves. Stir and cover. Steep for 30 minutes then strain out all the herb parts from the milk and proceed with your recipe.

If you add a bay leaf or two to your rice storage container, the rice will take on a nice flavor and maintain it when cooked.

❀ *Deter with it.* A bay leaf put into your flour bin will deter weevils. If you have a problem with ladybug invasions in your home during the winter, bay leaves will run them out without hurting them. Put some leaves or a wreath near doors and windows or wherever you see the little darlings and they will go back outside to find another home.

❀ *Dry it.* Add bay leaves to potpourri. Their smell, evergreen nature, and shapely leaves add texture and interest to any mixture.

❀ *Decorate with it.* Bay wreaths are not just for athletes and poets anymore. Bay leaves are perfect for making decorative wreathes at any time of the year, but they are particularly nice during the holiday season. Since they are evergreen, they will keep their dusky green color for a long time. A bay wreath is a wonderful gift for a fellow cook, especially if you add some garlic, peppers, or other culinary herbs as decoration. Be sure all your herbs are grown organically and that there is nothing toxic in the wreath. Attach parts with pins rather than hot glue. You can make your bay wreath any size—large for the door, small for party favors. In addition to the nice look, the wreath will add a subtle clean scent to the house.

✿ *Soothe with it.* Bay leaves are known in the medicinal herb trade as a soothing, sedating, and suppressant herb. A decoction added to bath water is said to relieve aching limbs and help people relax after a long day. A traditional tea of bay leaves known as "Italian Grandmother's Cure" was used to calm colicky babies and was thought to be good for anyone who had a gassy or upset stomach. A home remedy known as "gripe water" is made by placing 1 bay leaf in 1 cup of cold water in a saucepan. Brought to a boil and then simmered for about 3 minutes, the water is cooled a bit but drunk before it gets cold. Note: Other "gripe waters" can be made from dill or fennel seeds.

Bergamot *Monarda didyma*

☀ *Learn about it.* Bergamot, bee balm, monarda, Oswego tea, and several other common names identify this popular herb. The names come from its different characteristics. "Bergamot" refers to the Italian orange of the same name that has a similar scent. "Bee balm" comes from the fact that bees love this plant and will travel quite a distance to sip its nectar. "Monarda" comes from the scientific name, and "Oswego tea" refers to the tea made and used by the Oswego Indians and other tribes of Native Americans who used the tea as medicine for centuries. A native of North America, bergamot has several wild varieties—*Monarda fistulosa* and *M. punctata* among them— that share common names such as wild bergamot, horsemint, mountain mint, and others. All of the monardas can be used, but the most beautiful and tasty is the *M. didyma.*

During the American Revolution, loyalists drank home-grown bergamot tea instead of highly taxed China tea from Britain. Especially after the Boston Tea Party of 1773, the bright red flowers were grown as a highly visible sign of support for the American rebels and the beverage became known as Liberty Tea.

✹ *Grow it.* Bergamot is a member of the mint family and is therefore easy to grow if given enough water and light. The bright red, lavender, pink, or white flowers are beautiful in the garden and make a great display in either sunny or partly shady spots. This perennial prefers a rich, well-drained soil and will benefit from periodic feeding with mild organic mixes containing seaweed and fish emulsion.

Plant bergamot near tomatoes to improve the growth and flavor of the tomatoes. Bergamot plants are very attractive to all beneficial insects including bees, bumblebees, butterflies, and others. The sweet nectar draws them from near and far, and as a result your whole garden will be better protected from pests. Hummingbirds also love this flower.

✹ *Eat it.* The flowers of the bergamot are beautiful garnishes to a wide variety of dishes. You can scatter the flowers in salads, especially fruit salads, and use their petals as a garnish for other dishes.

✹ *Drink it.* Oswego tea makes a tasty refreshment. Place 1 teaspoon dried or 1 tablespoon fresh bergamot leaves in a cup. Add 1 cup boiling water and let steep 3–5 minutes. Add honey for sweetness. The tea has a nice minty flavor. If you like the taste of Earl Grey tea, add leaves of bergamot to regular tea for the same flavor. (3 teaspoons bergamot leaves to 1 teaspoon China tea steeped for 5 minutes in 2 cups of water.) Leaves of the bergamot plant added to wine, lemonade, and other fruit drinks add a minty, fresh flavor. A hot drink of bergamot leaves steeped in milk is tasty and relaxing.

✹ *Cut it.* The flowers of the bergamot plant make wonderful cut bouquets. Combine them with other garden flowers or let them stand alone. They will look nice and add a pleasant scent to the air.

✹ *Dry it.* Bergamot flowers keep their color when they dry so they are good additions to dried arrangements, potpourri, and wreaths. Dry them by hanging a bunch upside down in a dry, shady spot. Strip the leaves and use them for tea. Use the flowers to decorate year-round.

✹ *Soothe with it.* Bergamot contains the powerful antiseptic thymol. As a result, it has been used for a long time as a medicinal herb to increase the flow of blood in the affected area and help soothe and heal. It has been known to act as an antipyretic, antiseptic, anti-inflammatory, antispasmodic, carminative, diuretic, digestive aid, menstrual regulator, and diaphoretic (promotes sweating). Its traditional use is to calm digestive problems such as nausea, indigestion, and vomiting. It was also used to reduce mucus and fevers by promoting sweating during bouts of cold or flu.

Infusions of this herb have also been used on the body. When applied to skin, it is said to clear the complexion and be good for rashes and aching arthritic joints.

Some people pour boiling water into a bowl containing bergamot leaves, make a tent over their heads with a towel to trap the steam, and then breathe deeply for a while. This steam inhalation is said to ease breathing for bronchial catarrh and sore throat.

Victor Z Martin
2006

Borage *Borago officinalis*

✸ *Learn about it.* According to most sources, borage is an extremely old plant. It is said to have originated around Aleppo, a Syrian city that dates back to the eleventh century B.C. From there, it spread throughout Europe and was brought to the New World by early settlers. Historically, borage was thought of as an herb that would dispel depression and fear. It was consumed in wine by Roman soldiers to make them brave, and Pliny the Elder wrote, "it maketh a man merry and joyful." More modern writers attribute the great results of borage to the wine it was drunk in rather than the herb itself. Still, it is a great herb to grow in the home garden because it has other skills besides the historic ones.

✸ *Grow it.* Borage is an easy-to-grow herb that is often overlooked in the garden. It likes rich soil but will do fine in moderate garden soil. It makes an attractive, sort of straggly, bushy plant with bright blue, star-shaped flowers that contrast nicely with the dark green leaves. It blooms throughout the spring and early summer and requires little care. Bright light and moderate water are just what this sturdy annual needs, although some protection from strong winds will help keep it from breaking or blowing over. Placing plants close together lets them lean on each other and protect each other from the wind.

✸ *Eat it.* Borage does not dry well for culinary use, so use it fresh during the spring and summer. Fresh borage leaves have a flavor that resembles cucumber. Finely chopped leaves can be added to soups and stews during the last few minutes of cooking. The leaves also can be cooked with cabbage leaves (two parts cabbage, one part borage). When cooked, the hairs on the leaves dissolve so you don't taste or feel them. Fresh flowers and leaves can be used in salad, dips, and cold soups as garnish. Select young, tender leaves that have not developed stiff hairs if you are using them raw. Chop fine and add, along with flowers, to garnish salads, dips, and cucumber soups. Candied borage flowers make attractive cake decorations. Candied Borage Flowers: Pick the flowers, each with a small stem, when they are quite dry. Paint each one with a lightly beaten egg white, using a water color paintbrush. Dust them lightly with fine sugar and set to dry on waxed paper in a warm place.

✺ *Drink it.* Borage flowers and leaves are the traditional decoration for gin-based summer drinks, and freezing borage flowers in ice cubes to float in summer drinks or punch is a fun variation. Borage added to wine cups is a tradition, but you can also make borage lemonade if you don't want to be quite so "merry." Borage Lemonade: ¼ cup lemon juice, 2–3 tablespoons sugar, 3–4 medium sized borage leaves, 2 cups water. Put all ingredients in a blender and blend for about 30 seconds. Strain and serve over ice garnished with a borage flower.

✺ *Attract with it.* Borage is a great companion plant. It encourages beneficial insects to come into your garden and pollinate plants and eat pests. It also will improve the taste of tomatoes if it is planted near them, as well as discourage worms. Squash and strawberries also benefit from borage growing nearby.

✺ *Cut it.* Fresh borage flowers will add a nice hue to cut arrangements.

✺ *Dry with it.* Dried flowers can be added to potpourri to give a lovely blue color.

✺ *Soothe with it.* A poultice of borage leaves has been used for inflammation and bruises. Drinking tea made with borage is said to help reduce fevers and ease chest colds, flu, and cough. A simple folk recipe for borage tea involves adding a small handful of fresh borage leaves to 1 pint of boiling water. After simmering covered for 5 minutes, the mixture is strained and served. The tea may also be a good blood purifier and a general tonic. Both the leaves and flowers are rich in potassium and calcium.

VictorZMartin
2007

Burnet *Sanguisorba minor*

☀ *Learn about it.* Brought to the United States by the Pilgrims, salad burnet (or just "burnet") soon found a home in many colonial gardens, including that of Thomas Jefferson. Jefferson not only grew it in his garden but also had it planted in the fields to stop erosion and to provide forage for his livestock.

☀ *Grow it.* Salad burnet is a perennial herb with plump little leaves with scalloped edges. The flowers are very small and fairly insignificant. The plant grows happily in good to poor soil and requires little attention. It can be grown from seed or from transplants. Plant in full or partial sun and water until it is established. The herb quickly becomes drought-tolerant. Keep the flowers pinched off to encourage leaves to grow fuller. It is a good edging plant because it remains small and orderly. In most climates the plant is evergreen.

☀ *Eat it.* As the name implies, salad burnet is traditionally used in salads. Pick leaves when they are young and tender. Older leaves tend to be tough and often have lost their delicate flavor. The leaves' mild cucumber taste adds a nice flavor to green salads composed of any lettuce, cabbage, or other green.

Blended into cream cheese with other herbs, salad burnet makes a quick snack to serve drop-in guests. It goes well with borage, dill, thyme, oregano, and chives. Use it as a garnish and flavor enhancer in chilled tomato or vegetable juices or in Bloody Marys or other summer beverages. The leaves are also attractive garnishes and are good in butters, cheese dips, cheese balls, and in salad dressings. A nice herbal vinegar can be made of the leaves and used on fish or vegetable dishes. The vinegar also makes a great salad dressing when blended with oil.

Salad Burnet Vinegar: Put a generous handful of salad burnet in a quart jar and cover with white vinegar. Let it sit for a week or more, shaking occasionally. Taste the vinegar and, if it suits you, strain and use. If you want a stronger taste, leave it for a while longer. Use in dressing and with fish.

Salad Burnet Salad Dressing: ¼ cup salad burnet vinegar, ¾ cup olive or your favorite oil, salt and pepper to taste. Stir, whisk, or shake until blended well. Serve on salad.

Salad Burnet Butter: 3 ounces butter, 1½ tablespoons chopped salad burnet, 1 tablespoon chopped spearmint, salt, pepper, and lemon juice to taste. Combine and simmer for 10 minutes. Pour over grilled fish.

✵ *Soothe with it.* Salad burnet's big brother *Sanguisorba officinalis* is often called medicinal burnet, but salad burnet has all the same properties. It is full of vitamin C, and chewing the leaf may be good for an upset stomach or that too-full feeling you sometimes get after a meal. An infusion of the whole plant is said to be good for treating hemorrhoids and diarrhea. Some people rub an infusion of the leaves on the skin to soothe sunburn and other skin problems.

✺ *Tan with it.* Not many of us tan leather these days, but if you want to, the root of salad burnet is packed with tannin and has been used historically as a preparation to protect and process raw leather.

Victor Z. Martin
2006

Calendula *Calendula officinalis*

✹ *Learn about it.* Calendula, also known as pot marigold, is an old herbal flower that has been used for centuries in a variety of ways. Its yellow and orange flowers are a familiar sight in cottage gardens. It flourishes in cool temperate climates.

Some traditional herbalists insist that pot marigold is the correct name for this plant. The rest of us call it calendula because it is less confusing than calling it the name of another plant.

✹ *Grow it.* In many parts of the southern United States, calendula is a winter flower. It often grows alongside pansies throughout the winter months. Planted in late summer or early fall, it will produce flowers from early spring into summer. Some years it will continue to flower almost year-round.

Plant seeds in good garden soil and keep the soil moist until the plants appear. Since it grows in cooler weather, calendula does not usually require a lot of extra watering. Plant it in full sun and watch it grow. It is rarely of interest to pests. When the plant is stricken by high heat, simply pull it up and consign it to the compost heap. Plant a new generation the next fall.

Grown in the vegetable garden, calendula encourages pollinators and other beneficial insects.

✹ *Cook with it.* The petals with their slight aromatic bitterness are used in fish and meat soups, rice dishes, salads, and as a coloring for cheese and butter. The whole flower can be used as a garnish. The bright yellow flowers are sometimes used as a substitute for the very pricy saffron. Cook them with rice and your guests will swear you used the real thing.

★ *Make wine out of it.* You can find recipes on the Internet for "marigold wine," and calendula is the flower of choice for this concoction. It makes a clear wine with a clean, sharp taste.

★ *Cut it.* The flowers make an attractive bouquet alone or in addition to other garden flowers for cut arrangements. Since they bloom when most other garden flowers are dormant, they are a welcome addition to brighten your home.

★ *Get pretty with it.* Make an infusion of the flowers to use as a rinse to lighten and brighten hair. Make a cleanser by mixing crushed dried flowers into olive or almond oil. Creamy Calendula Cleanser: Warm 4 tablespoons olive or almond oil in a bowl placed over a saucepan of hot water. Stir in 2 tablespoons dried or fresh calendula flowers and heat gently for 30 minutes. Remove from heat and allow to cool. Stir in a few drops of violet, orange blossom, or rose water if you want a scented cleanser. Use this to cleanse the skin and add moisture and brightness to the complexion.

★ *Soothe with it.* Calendula is an antiseptic and was used during the Civil War to staunch bleeding and heal wounds. Some people make a cream or tincture from the flowers to use on sores, acne, and diaper rash. As an antifungal, it has been used to treat athlete's foot, ringworm, and candida. You can find calendula cream in health food stores. A similar cream is sometimes made at home by crushing dried flowers into a bland cream or ointment.

★ *Color with it.* Calendula flowers are often used as herbal dye. They dye wool a nice yellow color and have also been used to color butter, custards, and liquors. If you feed your hens calendula flowers, the resulting eggs will have a deep yellow yolk.

Victor Z. Martin
2007

Catnip *Nepeta cataria*

❀ *Learn about it.* Known as catnip, catmint, catnep, catswort, and field balm, this popular herb is most famous for its effect on cats (hence its common names). Yet, from Europe to China, catnip has been used as a medicinal herb for at least two thousand years. Early colonists brought it to America, and the Native Americans adopted it as a useful herb with some peculiar characteristics. Early Americans believed that catnip would make even the kindest person mean. It was traditionally used by hangmen prior to an execution to help them "get into the right mood." This tradition was soon forgotten, and catnip then became known only as an herb well-loved by the feline population.

❀ *Grow it.* Catnip is a hardy perennial that grows well in sun or partial shade. It is a good border or edging plant because of its mannerly habit. It will grow to 2–3 feet tall and produce nice blue flowers. Butterflies like the flowers, as do other beneficial insects such as bees. That makes it a good companion to vegetables and fruit that rely on bees for pollination. A member of the mint family, catnip has gray-green fuzzy leaves with a square stem.

✸ *Deter with it.* Catnip plants will help deter flea beetles, aphids, Japanese beetles, squash bugs, ants, and weevils. Sprigs in the house or garage will deter mice and ants.

Studies have shown that catnip repels mosquitoes more effectively than DEET, the traditional chemical compound used in insect repellants. Iowa State University Research Foundation acquired a patent for a catnip mosquito repelling compound in 2006, but the use of catnip to repel mosquitoes has been common in folk medicine for generations. Here are two popular recipes:

Mosquito Spritz: 2 cups catnip leaves, 3–4 cups mild rice vinegar. Rinse herbs, dry, and crush, then place in a clean quart jar and cover with vinegar. Seal jar and store in a dark cupboard for two weeks. Shake jar lightly every day or so. Strain into a clean jar, seal and refrigerate for up to 6 months. To use, pour a small amount into a spray bottle and spritz on exposed skin and around outdoor dining area.

Catnip & Rosemary Mosquito Chasing Oil: 2 cups catnip leaves, 1 cup rosemary cut into 6-inch sprigs, 2 cups grapeseed oil or any light body-care oil. Crush herbs and pack into a clean jar. Cover with oil, seal jar, and place in cool dark place for two weeks, shaking jar every day or so. Strain into clean jar, seal, and refrigerate up to 8 months. To use, rub on exposed skin.

✸ *Thrill cats with it.* Catnip is beloved by most cats. They like to roll in it, lick it, eat it, and generally give it a good mauling. Cats love the smell of the plant, and all that carrying on releases the essential oils that contain the scent. The cats who love it (and some pay it no attention at all) seem to go into a state of ecstasy when they are around the plant. A really enthusiastic cat can wipe out your plant. To try to preserve the garden, you can dry catnip and sew it into cat toys. Small balls, sachets, or mice made of cloth and stuffed with dried catnip are traditional feline toys. You can also stuff a sock (whose mate the drier has eaten) with dried catnip. Loop a heavy elastic band around the top and hang from a door knob. Hours of fun will ensue!

✸ *Soothe with it.* The leaves of catnip were once chewed for toothache and smoked to treat bronchitis and asthma (or by old hippies who would smoke anything). Catnip tea was used for centuries as a calming brew. It is said to soothe upset stomachs, menstrual misery, coughs, and act as a general tranquilizer. This tea is typically made by pouring 1 cup boiling water over 1–2 teaspoons catnip leaves, covering it and allowing it to steep for 15 minutes. The catnip itself is not boiled because that would dissipate its beneficial properties.

Chamomile *Chamaemelum nobile*

✤ *Learn about it.* Chamomiles are a bit confusing. There are several plants that have similar common names and appearances but whose growth habits and botanical characteristics are different. *Chamaemelum nobile* (also known as Roman chamomile, English chamomile, Hungarian chamomile, common chamomile, and even German chamomile) is a perennial plant with a distinctive apple scent. *Matricaria recutita* (also known as German chamomile—now you see the problem—and wild chamomile) is an annual plant. Then there is the stinking chamomile (*Anthemis cotula*), another annual that grows wild and lives up to its name. *C. nobile* is the true chamomile, and the others are known as "false chamomile," but we typically grow them all and call them all chamomile. Whew!

To make matters more confusing, it was a German botanist in the mid-sixteenth century who proclaimed that *C. nobile* was Roman chamomile. The Egyptians, Greeks, and Romans all used this small plant. Its cheerful yellow and white daisy-like flowers and sweet apple scent made it useful for a variety of purposes. The Egyptians identified the bright yellow center with the sun and dedicated the plant to their sun god, Ra. The Romans who collected the plant during their conquest of Britain planted it widely and used it generously as medicine and tonic, landscape material, and a bath herb.

✸ *Grow it.* Roman chamomile (*C. nobilis*) is the perennial form of chamomile, but in keeping with the confusing nature of this plant, it often grows as an annual in very hot and/or humid areas of the country. It prefers cool weather and will grow and prosper in the South and Southwest during the late fall, winter, and early spring, only to give up the ghost in hot summer weather. It is easy to grow from seed or from transplants. It should be planted in the fall or very early spring in most parts of the country. It will reseed easily and keep the plot going, even if it is not truly perennial in warm areas. Roman chamomile grows to about 6 inches tall and sprawls. It can grow in full or partial sun and is often used as a ground cover in cool areas.

German chamomile (*M. recutita*) likes the same conditions and is an annual that often reseeds. It does not have the strong apple scent of the true chamomile, but the flowers of both plants are used medicinally and as decoration. German chamomile blooms more freely than the Roman and is often grown just for the flowers.

The English often use Roman chamomile as a green divider between paving stones and in pathways. The plant is tough enough to take foot traffic. In areas of the United States where the weather is cool and the humidity is low, this is a good landscape use of the plant. It grows 3 or 4 inches tall and makes a good front-of-the-border plant where you would like a nice fragrance.

Chamomile is host to hoverfly and beneficial wasps, and it improves the flavor of cabbage, cucumbers, and onions. It is a general tonic for everything growing nearby in the garden.

✸ *Fight fungus with it.* An infusion made of 2 cups boiling water poured over ¼ cup chamomile flowers and steeped until cool can be sprayed on plants to prevent and help kill fungal infections in the garden. Put the liquid in a spray bottle and spray directly on problem areas. It is good for preventing damping off in seedlings and also to use on a seed bed when starting seeds. Soaking seeds in this infusion before planting will help the seeds come up strong and fungus-free. Chamomile is a concentrated source of calcium, potash, and sulfur. Sulfur is a natural fungus fighter.

★ *Soothe with it.* Who has not heard of the benefits of a nice cup of chamomile tea? The tea is made from the flowers of the plant, particularly the yellow center since the white rays usually fall off. The dried blossoms are often steeped in boiling water for 10 minutes at a rate of 1 cup boiling water to 2 teaspoons flowers, then strained and served. The tea is said to soothe, relax, and invigorate. Different types of chamomile have slightly different flavors, but all are believed to be equally beneficial. It is a mild sedative used by some for calming rattled nerves. It has also been used to soothe teething babies. It is generally very safe to use.

CAUTION: Some people with ragweed allergies have found they are also allergic to chamomile.

Chile Peppers *Capsicum* spp.

Victor Z Martin
2007

✱ *Learn about it.* Chile peppers come from America and were "discovered" by Christopher Columbus when he was searching for black pepper, the most expensive spice in the world at that time. So, of course, he called the spicy berries he found in the New World—peppers! The people of Peru and other South and Central American countries had been growing and using peppers for centuries before the Europeans showed up, and it did not take the newcomers long to discover just how tasty these little pods can be. Although Europeans were suspicious of other Native American plants like tomatoes, they welcomed peppers with open arms. Within fifty years of their leaving the shores of the New World, peppers had been incorporated into the cuisines of not only Europe but also India, China, and Africa.

Archeologists have found pepper remains in pottery in Oaxaca and Puebla in Mexico that date from 3000 B.C. It appears these peppers were cultivated rather than collected wild because the archeologists have found earlier examples that are small and sort of ragged and later examples that are larger and healthier.

Botanical classification is supposed to be helpful in distinguishing plants, but sometimes the scientific names are just confusing. Most edible peppers are of the species known as *Capsicum annuum,* which indicates that they are annual plants. Of course, almost all peppers are annuals, so that is not much help. Peppers of this type range from sweet to really hot. The second largest type of pepper is *C. frutescens,* which means that the plants are shrubby or bushy. These peppers have a compact habit and rarely grow more than 4 feet tall. Varieties of this species are usually pretty hot and include the tabasco pepper, which is very hot. A smaller group of chiles is called *C. chinense,* which would seem to indicate that the pepper came from China, but of course it did not. A botanist in the seventeenth century thought they came from China and gave them this name. This species includes varieties such as the habanero pepper, commonly accepted as the hottest in the world. Another group of peppers, *C. pubescens,* is believed to be the oldest domesticated species. Grown in Bolivia since about 6000 B.C., this pepper has a large fruit that is very hot. It is still mostly grown in high mountain regions of the tropics and is the only group of peppers that no longer has surviving wild relatives. *C. baccatum* includes all the peppers commonly referred to as Aji (pronounced Ah-Hee). These peppers also come from Bolivia, or perhaps Peru, and are hot but fruity flavored. Their name, which means "little" in Spanish, comes from the fact that the berries are rather small (not, as you might suspect, because eating them might tempt you to say "AHHHH EEEEE!"). They are also often yellow but sometimes can be purple or perhaps red or orange. There are also other groups of chiles, including wild peppers, which I won't go into here. The point is that names and classification of peppers are tricky because there are so many of them. And, there are more all the time. Peppers generally cross pollinate easily, creating new varieties whether you want them to or not.

The heat in chile peppers is measured by the Scoville Units scale. Sweet bell peppers measure at 0 Scoville Units. The habanero pepper ranges from 100,000 to 300,000. The heat in peppers comes from capsaicin, a chemical present in peppers to varying degrees. Measured by itself, capsaicin registers at 15,000,000 to 16,000,000 Scoville Units.

Chiles are not just hot, though. They are also good for you. The first isolated and identified vitamin C was found in paprika pods by

Hungarian chemist Albert Szent-Gyorgy, who won a Nobel Prize for his work in 1937. Regarding his discovery, he said, "Discovery consists of seeing what everybody has seen and thinking what nobody has thought."

✺   *Grow it.* One problem with chiles is that the heat varies greatly from plant to plant, even from pod to pod on the same plant. So, when picking a pepper to grow, find one you like most of the time and don't worry too much about Scoville Units. Peppers are easy to grow. They like good soil, hot sun, and enough water to keep growing. Their growth habits are much like tomatoes and other common garden vegetables. They should be planted outside in full sun once all danger of frost is past and fed good all-purpose organic fertilizer to keep them growing. They will produce fruit as soon as the plant is mature, but they really come into their own in the fall, producing lots and lots of beautiful shiny pods in a nice array of colors.

The biggest problem is deciding which varieties to plant. If you want to save seeds, remember to separate hot and sweet varieties because they cross easily—and every pepper that results as a cross between a hot and a sweet pepper will be hot. Peppers need to be pollinated by bees or other insects, so if you cover young plants to keep insects away, be sure to uncover them when they start blooming so they can be pollinated. Pepper plants sometimes need a little support when they are full of peppers. Growing them inside a tomato cage can help keep the plant from falling over or stems from breaking when it is heavy with fruit. Feed regularly; peppers seem to like a regular foliar spraying with liquid seaweed. Seaweed, which contains a wealth of trace minerals and some hormones, will also discourage pests and disease on the plants. Keep the pepper plants evenly moist. Harvest the fruit as it becomes mature to keep new fruit forming. Remember, annual plants think their work is done when they produce seed.

The chile pequin or bird pepper (or whatever other name you know it by) is a native, wild chile of the type *C. annuum* that is planted by bird droppings. It is a very small pepper that turns red when ripe and is very hot. This is one of the few perennial peppers that are common in home gardens. It comes back year after year without any effort from you. It also seems very happy in shady spots in the garden. The fruit of this pepper makes a great pepper vinegar.

✿ *Eat it.* The rage lately has been to see who can eat the hottest peppers. I don't quite understand this trend, but if you like it hot, there is a chile pepper for you. Chiles are essential for Mexican cooking and are also an integral part of the cuisines of India, China, the Southwest, and many other locations. Whole cookbooks, magazines, and organizations are centered around the uses and enjoyment of chile peppers. There is even a name for people who can't live without them—chile heads.

No salsa is complete without chile peppers, and no summer gathering is complete without salsa. Winter, on the other hand, demands steaming bowls of chili, a fragrant combination of chiles and meat.

Stuffed peppers are traditional fare in most cultures. The old standard—stuffed bell pepper with its filling of rice and meat—is still tasty, but you can let your imagination and your culinary skills soar by trying new filling for different peppers. If you like hot peppers, stuff one of them with cheese or rice or beans or potatoes or crab salad or anything that sounds good to you. Most experts say to roast and skin your pepper before stuffing. You can roast over an open fire or in the broiler, scorching the skin until it blisters and comes off easily. Do not rinse the peppers, just remove the skin and seeds and proceed. On the other hand, I like to stuff sweet peppers with the skin on, making the result firmer and easier to handle. I once stuffed peppers with leftover pork and rice chopped up with leftover squash medley (squash, onion, pepper, tomato), and it was delicious. Almost anything can be made into pepper stuffing, including a simple chunk of cheese.

Anytime you handle hot peppers, remember to protect yourself. Wear rubber gloves; do not rub your face and especially your eyes. That heat transfers easily and is concentrated in the white ribs and seeds that you often remove when preparing your peppers.

In addition to fresh peppers, you can also grow peppers that are great dried and ground. The most common of these is paprika. If you grow your own paprika, then dry and grind it, you will end up with something so much better than the brown stuff you buy at the store that you will think it is an entirely different spice. You can also make your own dried chili powder by combining ground dried hot chiles with other dried spices such as cumin and garlic. That way, you can get the taste you really like and also have a unique gift to share with friends.

Many peppers are used smoked or dried. Of course, just to keep us guessing, they are given different names after they are processed. So, Anaheim peppers become chile pasado when dried. Jalapenos become chipotle, and poblano peppers become ancho. Drying the peppers changes the flavor, and when they are added to recipes the result is quite different.

Pickled peppers and pepper vinegar are great ways to use excess peppers from the garden. Any pepper can be used in these ways. Pepper vinegar is good on cooked greens, fish, meat, and in many dishes. Pickled peppers go with anything!

✱ *Dry it.* You can dry your own peppers by making a small cut near the stem end and stringing the peppers on a thread. Hang the pepper necklace in a dry, shady spot. Use a needle to create your string of peppers and space them on the string so that they are not touching each other while they dry. Don't forget to wear your gloves if the peppers are hot.

If you have a dehydrator, you can dry your peppers in there by following manufacturer's directions. Remember that in humid climates the peppers will eventually rehydrate themselves and begin to rot. When that happens, just toss them in the compost heap and start on your next crop.

✱ *Decorate with it.* The long swags of dried chiles from New Mexico that we know as ristras are beautiful decorations in your home year-round. They are especially lovely in the kitchen. You can also get wreaths of chiles, either large or small, that are good for Christmas or anytime of the year. In New Mexico and other very dry areas, you can hang the ristras outside and enjoy them there, but in areas where the weather is humid or rainy, they will quickly soften and become moldy. They will keep longer in any climate if they are indoors. If you make your own ristras or know for sure what has been done to the peppers, you can pick off individual peppers and use them in cooking. If you buy a ristra in a shop, though, it may have been sprayed with something you do not want to eat.

You can also use your homegrown dried peppers to ornament wreaths. Added to a bay wreath or a rosemary wreath, peppers of red, orange, purple, or green make a beautiful decoration that can be used as well.

✸ *Soothe with it.* It is hard to imagine that something that hurts so badly can also make you feel better, but science is finding that the capsaicin in peppers has a stimulating and soothing effect on many hurtful conditions. Just look around the pharmacy and you will see lotions and potions that contain this strong chemical. It has been used for reducing pain from arthritis, aching joints, nerve pain, burning diabetic feet, and many other conditions. The capsaicin triggers the production of endorphins in the body, which helps everything feel better. (That endorphin-triggering effect is why we like to eat them even though they make our eyes water and our noses run.) The capsaicin also encourages blood to flow to the affected area, and healing is more apt to occur with good circulation. It depletes substance P, a neurochemical that transmits pain to the brain, so you feel better. While not a cure, capsaicin creams are used by millions of people to help them function with less pain. The cream is typically applied, while wearing gloves, directly to the spot that hurts. It may cause a temporary burning sensation, but that usually is mild and stops after a few minutes. Products made with capsaicin should be kept away from the face, eyes, mouth, and open sores.

Victor Z Martin 2005

Chives *Allium schoenoprasum*

✺ *Learn about it.* Chives are natives of China and are said to have been eaten by Marco Polo on his adventures. He reported their tastiness and brought a few back on his return to Europe, where they were widely accepted and cultivated. They now grow wild in many European countries. They have been used in cooking by the ancient Chinese for perhaps five thousand years. Romanian Gypsies are said to use chives to tell fortunes—how, I wonder?

✺ *Grow it.* Both onion (*Allium schoenoprasum*) and Garlic (*A. tuberosum*) chives are easy to grow. They can be grown in the ground or in containers with very little trouble. All they need is sunlight and a little water. In warm regions of the country, both are evergreen and you can use them year-round. In colder regions, it is easy to pot up a small cluster and keep it in the kitchen window for use during the cold weather, then plant it back outside when spring comes. Plant from seeds or from a division shared by a friend or use a transplant from the nursery. Once you have a start, it will keep going and going. If the plant begins to look ragged, give it a severe haircut and it will come back looking fresh and perky.

Onion chives have bright green, round, hollow leaves. Garlic leaves are also bright green, but they are flat and not hollow.

Chives make a wonderful garden border. Instead of planting monkey grass or liriope, plant something useful as well as decorative. Chives create a nice tumbling grassy border much like those ornamentals, but you can also eat them and they will encourage the growth of other plants in the garden. They bloom prettily in the spring and then provide a nice grassy edging to your bed. Be sure to clip off the flower heads of garlic chives before they go to seed or they will spread all over the garden like weeds. Onion chives are much less likely to reseed and become a nuisance.

★ *Eat it.* Snip the leaves of onion chives onto salads (green, potato, pasta, or cabbage), baked potatoes, fried potatoes, or anything else that needs a taste of onion. Be sure to cut the leaves all the way to the ground when harvesting. Generally, they will not grow back from the tip.

Garlic chives can be used to give any food a light garlic flavor. Snip the leaves as you would onion chives.

You can also use chives alone or combined with other herbs to create delicious herbal butters. Use them to butter bread, potatoes, steamed veggies, or in dishes that call for butter.

Add onion chive blossoms to salads or float them on top of soups. They are edible flowers that look beautiful on your table.

Both onion and garlic chives are best eaten raw or quickly cooked. Long cooking destroys their delicate flavors. They are popular additions to stir-fry recipes and egg dishes that are cooked rapidly. Add to other dishes just before serving. You can use the bulb of the garlic chive like a green onion, and the seeds can be saved and sprouted for a peppery addition to salads.

★ *Make vinegar with it.* Pack lovely pink onion chive blossoms in a decorative bottle then fill with white vinegar. White wine and rice vinegar are nice, but plain old white vinegar works fine. Let it sit for several days, shaking occasionally. The vinegar is delicious when used to baste baked or broiled fish, to serve as a condiment with fried fish or to flavor anything that benefits from a mild oniony taste. Chive blossom vinegar makes a wonderful salad dressing and is a pretty pink color. It is also a great gift when accompanied by a note telling how to use it.

★ *Deter with it.* Interplant onion and garlic chives with vegetables, flowers, around fruit trees, anywhere you want to repel pest insects. Chives can help repel pests and attract beneficial insects to the garden. Chives (along with other types of allium plants, such as garlic) are great companion plants for many other garden plants. They improve the growth and flavor of carrots and tomatoes. You can plant chives directly beneath roses and let their grassy plants and delicate flowers help protect the roses from pests, black spot, and other problems while they create a natural mulch at the same time. Planted near apple trees, chives help prevent scab. Take advantage of their scent to make your garden healthier, but keep them away from beans.

An infusion made of chives and sprayed on cucumber, pumpkin, squash, and other cucurbits will help prevent downy mildew, a fungal disease common to those plants. Put a bunch of chopped chive leaves in a container and cover with boiling water. Let the mixture sit until the water cools, then strain and spray. Use as often as twice a week until your plants are growing well and look healthy.

✸ *Decorate with it.* Both the pink onion chive blossom and the white garlic chive blossoms are lovely in fresh or dried arrangements. The scents are delicate and will not overpower any other flower, and the blossoms are not likely to shatter when dried. The pink blooms keep their color when dried and add a nice subtle hue to dried arrangements, potpourri, and wreaths.

Cilantro/Coriander *Coriandrum sativum*

Victor Z. Martin
2008

☀ *Learn about it.* Cilantro/coriander has been cultivated as a medicinal and culinary herb for more than three thousand years. It is mentioned in Sanskrit texts, Egyptian papyri, Hussain Haddawy's translation of *The Arabian Nights,* and the Bible. Spanish conquistadors introduced cilantro to Mexico and South America, where it became quickly associated with that cuisine. Also known as Chinese parsley, the herb has a long history in Chinese medicine and cuisine. One of the ancient uses was as an aphrodisiac. On the other hand, many people (including most Europeans) do not like the scent of this plant, and its name is said to come from the Greek word for bedbug because the plant smelled like those unpleasant creatures. Cilantro is a flavor that people generally love or hate.

☀ *Grow it.* Cilantro is easy to grow. The problem is that it often grows at the wrong time for most gardeners. We want it to be ready to pair with tomatoes and peppers, and it wants to grow in the cool weather long before tomatoes and peppers are ripe. In the South and Southwest, cilantro is a winter herb. It should be planted in the fall and enjoyed while the weather is cool. In cool climates it can be grown in the spring. No matter where you are, cilantro will be happy to bolt to seed at the first warm day.

Plant seeds in late summer and again in February to give your cilantro time to grow before the weather gets hot. It needs full sun and occasional watering if the weather is dry. Plant transplants any time the weather is nice enough to work in the fall and winter. A succession of crops will help your cilantro last longer.

On the other hand, if you let if to go seed you will have coriander, a fine flavor in its own right. If you do not harvest the seed, the plants will easily reseed and make new plants.

Grown in the vegetable garden, cilantro encourages pollinators and other beneficial insects. The plant is said to repel spider mites, aphids, potato beetles in the garden and spraying an infusion of cilantro will kill spider mites.

✺ *Let it ripen.* The seeds of the cilantro plant are known as coriander. An aromatic spice, coriander is used in sweets, cakes, breads, and to flavor liqueurs. You have to watch seed heads carefully because they ripen quickly. Cut just as the seeds begin to turn color and then hang the flowers upside down in a paper bag. The seeds will continue to ripen and drop into the bag.

✺ *Eat it.* Every part of this plant is edible. Cilantro leaves are a great addition to any salad. Cut fresh leaves and add to any other greens to give them the distinctive cilantro flavor. (Once the leaves get ferny looking or big and leathery, they have lost their fresh flavor, so toss them into the compost pile.) Combine cilantro with traditional cabbage slaw and you will have a new taste treat. You can use cilantro any time you would use parsley. You can make a pesto out of cilantro just as you would basil and freeze it for future use. If you enjoy the flavor of cilantro, don't limit your use of it to salsa.

Here is an easy and tasty dip that my daughter Jenny makes for every party: 1 pint sour cream, 1 packet of dried ranch dressing mix, 1 jalapeno pepper seeded and stemmed, and cilantro leaves. Whomp up in blender and see if you want to add more cilantro. If the dip is too thick, add milk to achieve the right consistency. This is good with raw veggies, crackers, or chips.

Coriander seeds are a traditional spice for Indian food. The seeds are lightly toasted and ground in a coffee grinder, then added to food. It is good in curries and other spicy dishes, but ground coriander also adds a nice fresh and slightly unusual flavor to cooked vegetables. You can also add it to fresh pestos made from many different herbs. Experiment and you will find this is an interesting and tasty herb in all its many forms. Roast and grind only a small amount of coriander seeds at a time. It quickly becomes stale and loses its fresh taste.

★ *Make salsa.* Everyone's favorite use of cilantro is in salsa. Combined with tomatoes, onions, peppers, and other flavors, cilantro makes the classic Mexican sauce for dipping or adding to cooked dishes. You do not need a recipe for salsa, just combine the ingredients in the proportions that suit you. Experiment with different kinds of peppers for a variety of tastes and heat. Chop it up or whir it in the blender. Cook it or leave it raw. Use tomatillos instead of tomatoes. This is not science. It is art!

If you live in a climate where the cilantro has not all gone to seed by the time peppers and tomatoes are ripe, you are lucky and can use your fresh herb in your salsa. In other climates, you will just have to go buy some cilantro at the store. There is no good way to keep it until the tomatoes are ripe in areas where the weather is hot.

★ *Cut it.* The flowers make an attractive bouquet or addition to other garden flowers for cut arrangements.

★ *Soothe with it.* Cilantro is traditionally used to settle the stomach and encourage good digestion. A poultice of the seeds is said to help with aching joints. The Chinese have used the herb in love potions and believed it will lead to long life. The essential oil of the plant contains antibiotic and fungicidal properties. Some say the seeds have cholesterol-lowering properties.

Victor L. Martin
2008

Comfrey *Symphytum officianale*

✸ *Learn about it.* Comfrey was for a while considered a miracle worker in the plant world. It was brought to England from the Middle East by crusaders who used it to heal the wounds of war. They called it Saracen's root. Known also as knit-bone and boneset, it was said to heal broken bones as well as almost any other injury.

CAUTION: For centuries it was taken internally (the leaves contain calcium, potassium, phosphorus, Vitamins A, C, B12 and other nutrients), but new research indicates it contains harmful alkaloids that should not be ingested.

✸ *Grow it.* Comfrey is a lovely plant that makes a big mounding clump of large leaves. The plant is 2–2½ feet tall and about the same width. It sends up a flower stalk of lavender, white, or pink bell-like blossoms. It is easy to grow and, once established, hard to get rid of. It grows from root divisions, and even the smallest piece can start a new plant. It is a great plant to share with friends and neighbors. Comfrey is happy in sun or partial shade. In the hot afternoon sun it tends to wilt but will perk right up when the heat diminishes a bit.

Plant comfrey in early spring from transplants or root divisions and keep watered until well established. It prefers good well-drained soil but is very tolerant of poor soil and even damp soil. Comfrey dies to the ground in cold winters but comes back quickly in the spring, even through a fairly heavy ground cover. During mild winters, the leaves may be evergreen.

Comfrey sends down a tap root that can grow as deep as 10 feet, which accounts for its ability to accumulate minerals, vitamins, and protein. It also helps loosen the soil with its extensive root system.

The leaves of the comfrey plant grow quickly, so you can harvest them many times in a season. Since they contain little fiber, they quickly compost and transform into nutrients for other plants.

✸   *Deter with it.* Comfrey is a good trap plant for snails and slugs. They like its large leaves and often take refuge under them. All you have to do is gather them up and dispatch them. Comfrey leaves are also helpful in preventing scab on potatoes. Plant a few wilted comfrey leaves with your potatoes, and the comfrey will help protect the young seedlings as they grow.

✸   *Fertilize with it.* Because comfrey leaves are so full of nutrients, they are a wonderful source of fertility for other plants in your garden. Adding leaves to your compost pile will make it rich in minerals and vitamins. You can also make an infusion and spray it on all your garden plants for a quick boost.

Comfrey Liquid Fertilizer: Pick a good sized handful of leaves. Cover with water in an outside container—a garbage can is good. Cover and let sit for 2 weeks. Squeeze the leaves and strain the liquid. Mix 1½ cups of this comfrey liquid with 1 gallon of water. Spray or drench the leaves and soil around your plants with the mixture. It will be quickly absorbed and will help your plants grow healthy and strong. Add the used leaves to your compost heap.

You can also use fresh comfrey leaves as mulch beneath other plants. They break down quickly and add their nutrients to the soil as they protect from extreme temperatures and maintain moisture in the soil.

✭   *Soothe with it.* Famed herbalist Dorothy Hall once suggested that the use of comfrey and garlic could almost halve the ailments in the western world—quite a claim! Comfrey leaves contain a substance called allantoin, which is a protein with hormone-like properties that stimulate cell growth and help repair and heal wounds, broken bones, burns, sprains, sore joints, dry skin, and swelling. Some people take advantage of this property by chopping fresh, clean comfrey leaves to make a poultice and wrapping it in a damp cloth. (Soaking the cloth in an infusion of comfrey doubles the effect.) The poultice is then applied to the hurt part as often as possible and left on as long as possible.

Comfrey has also been used as a poultice to treat septic sores on animals and as a feed for race horses.

Comfrey cream is usually available in health food stores and has been used for a variety of problems ranging from ringworm to poison ivy to broken bones. In fact, some people say if they hurt themselves while outside working in the garden, they just pick a comfrey leaf or two, wrap them around the sore spot, and by the time they get in the house it feels better.

Dill Anethum graveolens

✸ *Learn about it.* Dill weed is a native of the eastern Mediterranean area and western Asia, where it was highly prized as a flavoring and medicine. Egyptian medical texts mention it as far back as 3000 B.C. It was believed to protect people against witchcraft and was used as payment in the Bible. Romans considered dill good luck. Charlemagne made sure that dill was placed on his banquet tables so that guests who ate too much could chew it to settle their stomachs. The early settlers brought dill to America, where it was then widely grown. Children were given seeds of dill or fennel to chew in church to keep them quiet and both types came to be known as "meetin' seed."

✸ *Grow it.* Dill is an annual herb that is easy to grow. It prefers cool weather and will come to seed in early spring, so in warm climates it should be planted in the fall or late winter. It needs full sun, good garden soil, and sufficient water to keep it going. The newer hybrid varieties such as fernleaf dill will grow more compact plants and take up less room in the garden.

Dill is a good plant to help keep pests in the garden under control. It attracts hoverflies and predatory wasps. It is also a decoy plant for tomato hornworms, and most caterpillars love it. The beautiful swallowtail butterfly and caterpillar find dill irresistible, and you can lure them into your garden by growing it. They may eat more than their share of the leaves, so if you want some for yourself too, plant several!

Plant dill close to lettuce and cabbage to encourage their growth, but do not plant it near carrots or caraway.

Sprinkling leaves of dill on plants that are susceptible to squash bugs will help repel those pests.

✸ *Eat it.* Dill is a fresh tasting herb that combines well with many foods, but it should be used raw or added to dishes at the last minute because the oils are quickly destroyed by heat. The flower, leaf, and seed of the dill plant are all edible. The light ferny leaves are especially compatible with seafood. It is a very popular flavoring in Scandinavian cuisine, where fish is a basic element in any menu. Dill is particularly tasty combined with sour cream, yoghurt, and butter. Chop the leaf and add to salads, potatoes, meat, and fish.

The flower head is often used in pickling. It has a stronger flavor than the leaves and a fresher taste than dried seeds.

Dill Butter: Mince ¼ cup dill weed and combine with ½ cup softened butter. Mix well, cover, and store in the refrigerator for a couple of hours to let the flavor soak into the butter. Use with broiled seafood or as a spread for tasty crackers or breads.

Dill Dip: Combine nonfat yoghurt and nonfat cream cheese until it is the consistency you like. Add a finely chopped garlic clove, lemon juice, and a generous amount of chopped dill leaves. Mix well and serve with fresh veggies or crackers. This is easy and guilt-free, and probably even good for you if you eat it with veggies rather than crackers!

Dill seeds have a sharper flavor than the leaf and can be used ground or whole. Ground dill seed is a good salt substitute for those trying to lower their salt intake. It is flavorful and is compatible with most dishes.

✸ *Get pretty with it.* If your fingernails tend to be weak and unlovely, make an infusion of crushed dill seeds and soak fingernails in it. It will strengthen the nails and keep them healthy. Chewing the seeds is also a quick and easy way to ensure sweet breath.

✻ *Soothe with it.* "Gripe water," a traditional folk remedy intended to calm colicky babies, is sometimes made from dill or fennel seed by mixing 1 pint water and 1 teaspoon dill seed or fennel seed in a saucepan and simmering for 10 minutes. The liquid is then strained and cooled and used within 24 hours because it does not keep its potency beyond that time. This tea has historically been bottle-fed to babies at room temperature (or slightly warmed) to ease colic, encourage sleep, and treat hiccups.

A stronger tea made from 1 teaspoon dill seed to 1 cup boiling water is thought to be good for adults suffering from upset stomach. It has been used to help with indigestion, flatulence, hiccups, insomnia, and is said to stimulate milk in nursing mothers. Others gargle with it to ease sore throats and sores in the mouth.

My mother always sent us off to the refrigerator to take a swig of dill pickle juice to stop hiccups. It worked, too!

✻ *Stay healthy with it.* Dill is a very good source of calcium and also of dietary fiber, manganese, magnesium, and iron. In addition, dill also has an antibacterial quality that can help wounds heal and help keep bacteria from growing. That is one of the reasons that dill has traditionally been used to preserve food—pickles—because it keeps bacteria away and keeps the food safe for eating for a long time.

✻ *Save it.* Dill can be dried by hanging it in an airy, dry location, but be sure to put a paper bag around the seed heads to catch the seeds. The leaves and seeds can be dried and used in any recipe that calls for fresh. Leaves and seed can also be frozen, but leaves will likely lose their fresh green color once they thaw. The seeds can be eaten, and some can also be saved for planting next season in the garden. Pick the seed head before the seeds are ripe and let them ripen as they dry. Ripe seeds are toxic to some birds so it is best to get them out of the garden before they completely mature.

Victor Z Martin
2007

Epazote Chenopodium ambrosioides

☀ *Learn about it.* A native of Mexico, epazote is also called skunkweed, pig weed, wormseed, and goosefoot. Sounds pretty tasty doesn't it? Epazote is a wild plant that has been used in Mexican folk medicine for centuries. Ancient Aztecs used epazote both medicinally and as a culinary herb.

CAUTION: Use with care. Epazote is considered safe in small amounts, but is poisonous in large quantities. It also tastes bad in large quantities, so overuse isn't tempting.

☀ *Grow it.* As mentioned above, epazote is a weed and grows like a weed! You might want to grow it in a large container to keep it from sprawling all over the garden. It requires full sun and will do fine in poor soil with little water. Epazote is a shrubby annual plant that grows to about 3 feet in height. The seed heads turn a beautiful bronze color at the first frost in the fall. Because it is so common a weed, it is often hard to find seedlings in nurseries. Learn to identify it in the wild.

☀ *Suppress with it.* The main use of epazote is to control gas. You can do that by adding the leaves to beans as you cook them or by making a tea with the leaves. Remember to use a small amount (2–3 leaves).

✦   *Eat it.* Epazote is a popular herb in many Mexican and Caribbean dishes. It has a flavor all its own that can't be replicated with other seasonings. Its most common and popular use is as a seasoning for beans—black beans, pinto beans, any dried beans. It not only flavors the beans nicely, it helps keep them from causing gastric discomfort (gas).

Refried Beans: 2 cups uncooked dried pinto beans or black beans, 2 sprigs epazote, ½ cup bacon drippings or lard, 1 clove chopped garlic, 1 serrano chile, seeded and halved, salt to taste. Rinse beans and check for debris. Place beans in a large pot and fill with water. Add epazote. Bring beans to a boil, then reduce to a slow simmer for 2 hours. If water level gets low, add more water. When beans are very soft, heat lard or bacon drippings in a large skillet over medium heat. Cook the chile until browned. Remove and discard chile. Add garlic and cook briefly; do not brown. Gradually add about ½ cup beans at a time to the skillet, mashing them as you go and adding cooking liquid as needed to keep the beans from being too stiff. Once all the beans are mashed, add salt to taste.

Like cilantro, another Mexican herb, epazote is an acquired taste and some never acquire it. Devotees claim that it adds wonderful flavor to many dishes, particularly soups, shellfish, and eggs. It combines well with other Mexican seasonings such as cumin, chiles, and oregano. Experiment with a pinch or two of epazote the next time you are making a Mexican dinner.

✦   *Decorate with it.* The cut branches of epazote make a good wreath base. They are flexible when green, and the large leaves look good when dried. A bunch of epazote hung to dry also makes an attractive and effective room freshener.

Victor Z. Martin
2007

Fennel *Foeniculum vulgare dulce*

✸ *Learn about it.* Fennel in cultivation dates back to ancient Greece. The battle at Marathon in 470 B.C. was fought on a field planted with fennel, and for a while, the Greeks called the plant "Marathon." In Greek mythology, knowledge was given to man by the gods in the form of a burning coal on a stalk of fennel. Ancient Romans believed that chewing on fennel stalks would prevent obesity—and it probably did if that was all they chewed! In Medieval times, fennel was hung around the house to keep out ghosts and evil spirits and to bring good luck. Like dill, fennel was used by Puritan Americans as "meetin' seeds" to chew during long, tiresome sermons.

✸ *Grow it.* There are three main types of fennel: Florence fennel, which has an enlarged bulb and is used as a vegetable; wild fennel, which is bitter and of little use; and sweet fennel, which is a valuable and tasty herb. Sweet fennel is available in green or bronze types. Both colors have the same growth pattern, same flavor, and same characteristics. The only difference is the color.

Both bronze and green fennels are tall, ferny plants that produce tasty fruits that are generally referred to as seeds. The whole plants are edible and have a mildly licorice flavor. Mature plants grow to 4 feet tall and are good container plants since they are said to inhibit the growth of other plants in the garden. They are not picky about soil but do like full sun and good drainage. Do not plant near dill, parsley, carrot, or other close relatives because they cross pollinate easily and the result is that none of them are tasty.

Fennel can be planted either in early spring or in the fall. It is winter hardy in most areas. If you plant it in containers, be sure they are large enough to accommodate fennel's long taproot. Plant seeds about ¼ inch deep in lightly moist soil. Fennel requires minimal water, and the flavor is concentrated when it grows on the dry side. Watch closely to harvest the seeds before they fall on the ground. Dry the plant hanging upside down and catch the seeds in a brown paper bag as they fall.

Fennel is perennial in most areas, or at least biennial. When the plant has finished blooming and you have harvested the seeds, cut the stalks down to ground level and let it start over again.

✹ *Eat it.* All parts of the fennel plant are edible. The leaves and stalk make wonderful flavoring, especially for fish, and the seeds are a tasty addition to many dishes including sausage. Add fennel leaves to salads and use as garnish on any plate. The delicate leaves are particularly attractive when bunched around meat or beside veggies.

Fennel Butter: ¼ cup softened butter, 2 tablespoons chopped Fennel leaves, 2 teaspoons lemon juice, salt and pepper to taste. Combine and refrigerate. This butter is particularly good on grilled or baked fish.

Chinese Five-Spice Powder: 1 tablespoon black pepper, 1 tablespoon ground anise, 1 tablespoon ground fennel seeds, 1 tablespoon ground cinnamon, 1 teaspoon ground cloves. Mix and store in an airtight container.

✹ *Attract with it.* Swallowtail butterflies and caterpillars *love* fennel. If you want these beautiful butterflies in your garden, plant fennel. The caterpillars with fat yellow and black bands on their green bodies are great looking creatures in your garden. Be warned that they can strip your plant, so if you want lots of butterflies and fennel too, plant lots of fennel. Start harvesting leaves before the caterpillars arrive.

✹ *Soothe with it.* Fennel tea is thought to be good for indigestion, gas, and colic, as well as colds, coughs, and sore throats. The tea is typically made by crushing 1 teaspoon fennel seeds and steeping in 1 cup boiling water for about 10 minutes. It is also said to curb the appetite and help with weight loss efforts.

Victor Z Martin
2007

Feverfew Tanacetum parthenium

✸ *Learn about it.* Feverfew is an ancient herb that is native to southeastern Europe. It was used by the ancient Greeks as a healing herb. According to Plutarch, its name "parthesum" comes from its having saved a man's life after he fell while working on the construction of the Parthenon (477–432 B.C.). In the Middle Ages, people in England bound bunches of feverfew on their wrists to keep away disease.

✸ *Grow it.* Feverfew is sometimes mistaken for chamomile, and they do look quite a bit alike. Both have small white daisy-like flowers with yellow centers, and both plants grow fairly low to the ground. Feverfew has flat flowers, and the plants grow to about 2 feet tall. They are easy to grow and reseed easily in dry, well-drained soil. They prefer cooler weather and will often die back in the middle of summer in high heat. They make good container plants and combine well with other plants in mixed groupings.

✸ *Deter with it.* Flowers and leaves of the feverfew plant can be dried and put into sachets to help repel moths in clothing. Put them in drawers, chests, and closets. Bees do not like this plant, so it is good to use near openings of the house where you don't want bees coming in. Do not plant it near food crops that need bees for pollination. It is said that a handful in a pocket is enough to keep bees away if you are walking outside where they congregate and are worried about bee stings. One person planted it in a hanging basket near a hummingbird feeder to keep bees away from the nectar in the feeder.

* *Cut it.* The fresh flowers with their bright daisy-like appearance add cheer to any small bouquet or arrangement.

* *Dry it.* The leaves and flowers hold their scent well even after drying. Use them in potpourri or just by themselves in a lovely bowl on a table to freshen and scent the room.

* *Soothe with it.* Although the name "feverfew" refers to the plant's ability to reduce fever, it has rarely been used for that purpose. Instead, it is most commonly used to soothe aches, stomach spasms, arthritis, and other pains. Unlike many herbs, feverfew has actually been widely tested as a medicinal, particularly as a treatment for migraine headaches. In some tests it was shown to reduce and prevent migraines as effectively as—and frequently more effectively than—modern medicine. It has also been tested as a relief for rheumatoid arthritis. A tea of leaves and flowers has been said to ease upset stomachs and menstrual complaints. Most sources say there are few negative side effects of this herb, but as with any herb, be sure to research it thoroughly before ingesting it.

Victor Z Martin
2005

Garlic *Allium sativum*

✸ *Learn about it.* No other herb has served as many roles in the culinary, medical, and folkloric histories of so many cultures as garlic. An Egyptian medical papyrus from the sixteenth century B.C. lists twenty-two remedies employing garlic for everything from heart disease and worms to tumors, headaches, and bites. Ancient Olympic athletes chewed garlic to build strength and stamina, and for centuries the Chinese have drunk garlic tea to relieve fevers, cholera, and dysentery.

The culture of garlic is so ancient that no one knows where the plant first originated. Virtually every culture has used garlic from time immemorial, both as a food and as a healing plant.

✸ *Grow it.* Garlic is easy to grow. It will sprout in almost any soil and grow happily in both sun and partial shade. Many fruit growers plant garlic among their trees for its protective properties, and it grows well under and around the trees. Plant garlic in the fall for best results. In areas where the ground does not freeze, you can plant garlic any time from September to March. If you have cold winters, plant either in September or October or as early in the spring as you can work the soil. The plant is extremely frost-hardy, but it needs time to grow some roots before the soil freezes, so try to get it in the ground six to eight weeks in advance of a deep freeze. Garlic is very forgiving, so you can plant it in early spring, but the bulbs will be smaller and the plants less vigorous. Select a clove of a garlic you like and plant it with the end pointed up. Try to find garlic that has been grown organically. A farmer's market or grocery that specializes in untreated food is a good source, as are friends and neighbors who grow garlic. More and more garlic at grocery stores comes from China and has little flavor. Grocery store garlic is also often treated with chemicals to keep the bulbs from sprouting. You want them to sprout! There are several mail order catalogs that offer broad selections of garlic bulbs. Experiment with different ones to see which you like best. You can also find garlic growing along the roadways in many areas. This wonderful "ditch garlic" is often very tasty and has escaped from old homesteads to grow wild. Just be sure it really is garlic when you dig it up. The smell test is all you need. If it smells like garlic, it is!

Garlic will grow in almost any kind of soil. Like most other plants, however, it will grow better in better soil. Garlic flourishes best in a rich, moist, sandy soil. Soil to which organic matter has been added and which has been loosened well will provide good growing ground for garlic.

Common garlic is a member of the same group of plants as the onion. The leaves are long, narrow, and flat like grass. The bulb develops underground into a cluster of bulblets, or cloves, that are held together in a sac of whitish skin. The flowers grow at the end of a stalk rising directly from the bulb and are generally whitish or lavender colored. Small bulbils grow among the flowers of some varieties creating a globe of blossom. The small bulbils in the flowers are not seeds, but they can be planted. Generally it takes a couple of years for a plant to result from these tiny bulbs. They can also be used as flavoring in recipes.

Select a sunny spot for your garlic bed (but the plants will grow in the shade of deciduous trees) and work compost, manure, or other organic material into the soil. Separate the cloves in the bulb right before you are ready to plant and plant each clove about 2 inches deep and the cloves about 6 inches apart. The small, pointy end of the clove should point up. Smart gardeners plant garlic all over the place—around fruit and nut trees, in the vegetable garden, in the flower beds—wherever they want to discourage pests. A layer of organic mulch on top of the soil will help keep the temperature moderated and the growing plants moist. Keep weeds down as much as possible and give the young plants a spraying of seaweed tonic once a month or so throughout the winter.

Some experts say that the flower stalk should be removed to make the bulb larger; others say the flower stalk should remain in place. If you want to avoid a hard core in the center of your bulb, remove the flower stalk. Many gardeners love the beauty of the flower, however, and don't mind a central core in the bulb. You can tell the garlic is ready to be dug when the flowers are fully open and mature or when the leaves begin to sag and yellow. The plants will mature anytime from May to September, depending on your location.

Each individual clove will produce a bulb containing many cloves. The planted clove will first sit quietly in the soil for a while, then send up green leaves that are attractive in the garden throughout the winter. In spring, a flower stalk will appear and that is a signal that the bulb is forming.

When you dig the bulbs, treat them as you do onions. Let them cure slowly in a spot where air circulates and where there is very little mois-ture. Hang the plants (stalk, flower, roots, and all) in a shed or other pro-tected spot. In a couple of weeks, the plants will be "cured" and ready to store. The bulb can be cut from the stalk and placed into containers that allow air to circulate (baskets are good). You can also freeze whole bulbs of garlic to be used later. One convenient way to preserve garlic is to peel and chop it in a food processor with a small amount of oil and freeze it in a plastic bag or glass jar. When you are ready to use it, simply dip out what you want and put the rest back in the freezer.

You can cut off the flower heads when you pull up the bulbs and dry them by hanging them upside down or by putting them in a dry vase or jar with air circulation. They will smell like garlic for a while but will dry naturally without your having to do anything. I dry them on the porch until the scent calms down a little.

As you begin to enjoy the flavor of your homegrown garlic, remember to save the fattest clove from each bulb to replant. If you select the best each year, soon your plants will be bigger and better than you ever imagined. As the plants become established, they will also form hard little bulbletes that often remain in the ground when you pull the bulb. These will make new plants, sometimes taking two years to form large plants, but soon your garlic patch will be self-sustaining and naturally vigorous.

There are two general kinds of garlic—the hardneck varieties and the softneck varieties. Hardneck garlics send up a central stalk that eventually matures into a cluster of flowers. Softnecks have evolved from the hardneck varieties and generally do not produce a flower stalk. The softnecks are easily braided and are valued for this characteristic. However, they are generally hotter in flavor than the hardneck types.

✤ *Experiment with it.* Garlic heat can range from very hot to mild. Like pepper heat, garlic heat is a very subjective thing. Some people don't think garlic is hot at all, while others shy away from its taste. It is fun, then, to experiment with different types and find the one that suits your taste. Any variety will produce better for you once you have grown it for a few years. Garlic adapts quickly to a location, and once established, it produces more flavorful and larger bulbs.

Rocambole (*Allium sativum* var. *ophioscorodon*) is a common variety of garlic that has been a source of a good deal of confusion. According to Marian Coonse in her book *Onions, Leeks & Garlic,* "Identification of this perennial has been confusing botanists since 1601." At one point, it was even named *A. sativum* var. *controversum.* Rocambole resembles common garlic except that it is a much larger plant. The flower stalk will rise to 3 feet or more, and the bulb is considerably larger than common garlic. The flavor is generally milder. Coonse describes the differences between common garlic and rocambole: "A distinguishing characteristic of rocambole is that as the stem rises above the leaves, it coils about itself, eventually straightening out again and continuing upward. A long, pointed green cap forms at the top of the flowering scape. As the buds open, the green cap falls to one side, exposing numerous tiny bulblets among the flowers." Rocambole is considered a hardneck garlic by commercial producers.

There are other plants that are related to garlic and that have garlic flavor, but are not, strictly speaking, garlic. Elephant garlic (*A. ampeloprasum*) is more closely related to the leek. It is, however, grown just like common garlic, except the plants should be placed farther apart. Society garlic and garlic chives also have the flavor of garlic; they are members of the onion tribe that produce leaves but no bulbs. Both add garlic flavor to cooking and serve to deter pests in the garden.

✸ *Eat it.* Garlic is one of the best flavorings around. It goes well with almost any kind of food—vegetables, meat, cheese, and almost any combination you can think of. Who can imagine Italian, Mexican, or American cuisine without it? Garlic is a great flavoring when combined with other herbs in mixes such as pesto, dips, and spreads.

Garlic becomes sweet when it is cooked and bitter when it is burned. When sautéing garlic, be sure to keep your heat low enough to avoid burning. Cook it until it is transparent but not brown.

There are complete cookbooks focusing on cooking with garlic. The Garlic Festival in Gilroy, California, has been celebrating garlic for more than twenty-five years and in that time raised millions of dollars for local charities. The garlic cook-offs have resulted in hundreds of innovative ways to use garlic in cooking. Everything from soup to desserts is created and the recipes collected in their own cookbook.

Since the Gilroy Garlic Festival began, other garlic festivals have sprung up around the country. Each offers new recipes and varieties each year and would be fun to visit.

If you want to have a handy, easy-to-use form of garlic, you can make your own garlic powder. It will be much better than the stuff you get at the store. Garlic Powder: Slice garlic bulbs thin and air dry. When completely dry, put into a plastic bag and pound vigorously with a hammer until the garlic is pulverized. This is a good tension reliever as well as culinary exercise.

Roasted garlic can be used as a great, simple spread on toast or crackers or added to recipes. Here's how: Remove as much of the paper from 2 whole heads of garlic as you can without breaking apart the cloves. Place garlic heads in ¼ cup water in a small baking dish. Drizzle with 1 tablespoon olive oil. Cover with aluminum foil or baking dish cover. Put into 375°F oven. Baste with olive oil/water mixture after 30 minutes.

Bake until garlic is soft and easily pierced with a thin-bladed knife, about 1 hour total cooking time. Slice off the top end of the bulb with a sharp knife, cutting through into the cloves. Roasted garlic can be squeezed out and spread like butter.

✸ *Deter with it.* In the garden, garlic is of great benefit in deterring pests. Almost every pest insect will run from the scent of garlic growing. Although people cannot generally smell garlic while it is in the ground, insects can, and that scent is enough to send them in another direction. Garlic has also been recommended to keep moles and other digging critters out of the garden.

Aphids are repelled by garlic. Growing garlic near or mingled with roses is said to ward off black spot. That is because the heat of the garlic comes from the plant's ability to accumulate sulphur, a naturally occurring fungicide. Many fungal diseases are prevented by growing garlic throughout the garden.

When used as a spray, garlic helps keep insects and diseases out of the garden as well. In *Organic Plant Protection*, Roger B. Yepson Jr. says that experiments on the use of garlic spray as an insecticide and as an antibiotic for controlling plant diseases showed that "garlic sprays effectively controlled downy mildew on cucumber and radish, cucumber scab, bean rust, bean anthracnose, early blight of tomato, brown rot of stone fruits, angular leaf spot of cucumber, and bacterial blight of beans."

A concentrated spray repels and kills whiteflies, aphids, fungus gnats, and other flying insects. It can be used on indoor and outdoor plants, even delicate plants such as orchids.

Garlic Spray: Mix 5 cloves of garlic with 2 cups of water in the blender. Blend well. Add a tablespoon of liquid soap and stir until dissolved. Strain into a sprayer that dilutes the mixture at a ratio of about 1 part garlic juice to 20 parts water or more. You can add hot pepper to this recipe plus a little mineral oil if you wish to add more punch. You can also add seaweed and fish emulsion to provide health benefits to your plants while you run off the bugs and disease. Spray on your plants, preferably in the early morning so it will dry before the sun gets really hot.

✸ *Stay healthy with it.* It is not just old folklore that attributes garlic with healing powers. Louis Pasteur described the antibacterial properties of garlic. Albert Schweitzer, deep in the jungle without mainstream pharmaceuticals, gave his patients garlic for amoebic dysentery. Garlic was in great demand during both world wars as an antiseptic. For example, during World War I, sphagnum moss was soaked in garlic juice to use as an antiseptic wound dressing. In 1916, the British government asked for tons of garlic bulbs, offering 1 shilling per pound for as much as could be produced. Medical studies of the efficacy of the plant continue.

According to a report in the *Journal of the American Medical Association* in 1990, more than one thousand scientific studies have described the therapeutic roles of garlic. In 1994, Adesh K. Jain of the Clinical Research Center at Tulane University School of Medicine reported that garlic may lower blood levels of total cholesterol and, particularly, of the dangerous low-density lipoprotein (LDL) form (so-called "bad" cholesterol). Studies in Germany have shown that garlic is a natural blood thinner and is beneficial to patients suffering from blood clots, particularly in the legs.

Benjamin Lau, researcher at the Loma Linda University School of Medicine, has identified three ways garlic protects against cancer. Other researchers have validated and expanded his studies about how garlic protects against cancer and precancerous conditions.

Garlic is said to be helpful in treating whooping cough and regulating blood sugar. It may guard against strokes. The list goes on and on, showing that garlic is beneficial to humans. But, the fact is that people love garlic—whether it is good for them or not!

According to uselessknowledge.com, Eleanor Roosevelt ate three chocolate-covered garlic balls every morning on the recommendation of her doctor. It was supposed to improve her memory. (My question is: where did she get chocolate-covered garlic balls?)

Geraniums (Scented) *Pelargonium* spp.

Victor Z. Martin
2007

★ *Learn about it.* Scented Geraniums are native to the Cape of Good Hope area in Africa and were introduced to British gardeners in 1632 by an intrepid sailor and plant collector looking for treasures for the courts of Europe. By 1847 the French perfume industry was using *Pelargonium graveolens* (rose geranium) in the production of rose-scented perfumes. The Victorians brought it indoors to scent rooms and placed it so that their long skirts brushed against it and activated the essential oils that give off the nice smells. When the plants were first discovered, there were said to be hundreds of different varieties. Now only about seventy-five remain, and some of them are newer hybrids.

★ *Be amazed by it.* Scented geraniums come in a wide range of fragrances. Among the most common are rose, ginger, lemon rose, peppermint, lemon, peach, balsam, nutmeg, peppermint rose, apple, strawberry, camphor, orange, and chocolate peppermint. The variety of scents is matched by the variety in appearance. Some geraniums are small leaved, others large. Some have scratchy, deeply cut leaves, others have smooth-as-velvet rounded leaves. Spending a day in a nursery full of these great natural mimics is a joy to anyone who loves plant oddities.

✺ *Grow it.* Although they are tender perennials, scented geraniums are easy to grow. Just don't leave them outside in the winter. If heavily mulched, they might come back after a mild winter, but it is best not to take the chance. They are great container plants as well as garden plants. In hot regions, they like a bit of afternoon shade to protect from the burning sun. They do like a lot of light, so bright shade is a good choice for them or a spot that gets morning sun and afternoon shade. Plant scented geraniums in rich garden soil or potting soil. Regular feeding with a weak solution of organic fertilizers will keep them growing steadily.

Scented geraniums tend to be leggy and tumble around on themselves. You can make them more compact with regular trimming. They bloom once in the spring, and generally the flowers are not very impressive. Unlike their cousins, the garden geraniums, with big bright flowers, scented geranium flowers are often subtle colors of white or lavender or pink and are small. The leaves are the interesting part of this plant because they contain the lovely fragrances.

If your scented geraniums are growing in containers, don't set the containers in saucers. The plants hate wet feet and will give you lots of problems if you over water them. Let the top of the soil dry completely before watering again.

Cut back your plant and bring it indoors as winter approaches. It will not survive even light freezes. If your plant is too big to bring in, take a cutting and grow it over the winter. Scented geraniums are easy to root. Simply cut off a growth tip, remove all the leaves except the ones on top and place the stem into good potting soil. Keep moist but not wet and give bright light. When it begins to grow, you know you have roots.

✺ *Sniff it.* Even though we do not wear big flouncy skirts like the Victorians did, we still like our homes to smell good. Scented geraniums are wonderful air freshening plants and their scents are released when you touch them or when someone bumps against them. Put them in a sunny spot near traffic if possible, so that they can be regularly urged into action with a gentle touch.

Scented geraniums also make good potpourri. Dry the leaves and crumble them into a bowl. Shake or toss it from time to time to release the scent.

Hang a bunch of leaves as an air freshener; put some crushed leaves on the floor and vacuum them up to freshen the air. You can also put a handful of leaves in a mesh bag and throw it in the drier with your linens for a nice, clean, lemony or rosy or minty smell.

✹   *Eat it.* Scented geranium leaves make a nice fragrant addition to cookies, cakes, butter, drinks and many other types of foods. You can add their subtle flavor to most sweets by sticking a few leaves into your sugar canister and letting the leaves infuse the sugar with their scent. Flavored sugar is also good added to hot or cold tea. You can also chop leaves and add them to your favorite plain cookie or cake recipe. One favorite way to use them is to place a layer of rose or lemon-rose (or your favorite flavor) scented geranium leaves in the bottom of a bundt or tube pan, then pour the batter for your favorite pound cake over them. When the cake is removed from the pan, the leaves are on top, making an interesting design and presentation for your guests—who more than likely will look with suspicion at what they see. Once you assure them that you didn't add oak leaves to the batter, they will delight in the unusual taste treat. You can vary the flavor by changing variety of geranium leaves and cake. Use lemon cake with lemon Geranium leaves; use orange with orange or with lemon; use rose with lemon; use mint with chocolate. Experiment and enjoy the results of your creative endeavors!

✹   *Drink it.* Scented Geranium Lemonade: Make a syrup of ½ cup sugar and 2 cups water by mixing and boiling until sugar is dissolved. Add 8 Scented geranium leaves and remove from heat. Cover and steep for at least 30 minutes. Strain the syrup into a pitcher and stir in ½ cup lemon juice and 4 cups water. Taste and adjust flavor to suit yourself. Chill and serve. You can also use this recipe to make lavender lemonade (2 tablespoons lavender flowers), rosemary lemonade (two 4-inch sprigs of rosemary), mint lemonade (½ cup fresh mint leaves) or basil lemonade (½ cup fresh basil leaves).

✺ *Relax with it.* Scented geraniums, with their variety of flavors and scents, are perfect for creating relaxing baths and drinks. You can make a sachet of crushed leaves and let the bath water run over it. The result will be a nice soothing soak with wonderful scents that linger.

If you are weary from the summer heat, try a Geranium Cooler to brighten your day and cool you off: In a teapot or other heatproof container, combine 6 leaves of rose geranium and 6 leaves of peppermint geranium. Pour two cups of boiling water over the leaves and let steep for 5 minutes. Sweeten to taste and cool. Strain and serve over ice for a relaxing and refreshing summer drink.

You can add scented geranium leaves directly into the teapot when you make regular tea. They will add a new flavor and aroma.

✺ *Get pretty with it.* Rose water is a common scent that has been used for centuries as a part of beauty regimens. The same wonderful smell can be achieved using rose geranium leaves. Combine a generous handful of rose-scented geranium leaves with 2 cups water and simmer for 15 minutes. Cool and strain. You can use this water as an astringent for your skin or a rinse for your hair. It leaves your hair shiny and smelling great. Rose water is also often combined with other components to make them smell good—rose water and glycerin for smoothing the skin, rose water in the bath for a subtle fragrance, rose water added to homemade soaps or hand lotions.

✺ *Make paper with it.* An old craft that is being revived is that of handmade paper. Scented geraniums are a popular addition because they add bulk, fiber, and scent to the paper.

Germander *Teucrium chamaedrys*

✺ *Learn about it.* Germander is a very old plant that has been used in formal gardens and in herb gardens to define the shape and the edges. Many knot gardens are outlined with germander because it is a very tidy and compact-growing plant. In the Middle Ages, germander was used as a medicinal herb. It was thought to cure gout and is credited with healing German emperor Charles V of that ailment in the sixteenth century. A tonic made of germander leaves was believed to have an all-around good effect on health and was drunk as a preventative for disease.

It was also used as a strewing herb, even though it does not have much fragrance. Instead it has lots of leaves that compacted nicely and could be absorbent on dirty and stinky floors of the castle where dogs, warriors, and other smelly animals hung out. When formal knot gardens became popular, germander became more popular as well. More cold-hardy than boxwood, the other common choice for knot gardens, germander is easy to maintain and looks nice with other herbs. George Washington grew germander in his knot garden at Mount Vernon.

✺ *Grow it.* Common or wall germander is an upright growing plant that has small, dark green scalloped leaves. The plant is a hardy perennial and evergreen so that it keeps its tidy appearance throughout the year. It grows about 1–2 feet tall and has nice pink to purple flowers in the early summer. The stiff branches of the plant form a dense hedge and can be clipped to maintain a standard height. It is ideal to grow around the edges of beds, along walkways, and as a defining element in a labyrinth or maze.

There is also a prostrate germander, which isn't really prostrate. The leaves are a duller green and its growth habit is about the same as wall germander, just a little looser—sloppier, some might say. It is the same height.

Germander is not picky about growing conditions. It is drought-tolerant, can take poor soil, and will thrive in sun or partial shade. Prune it to shape and size in the spring and whenever a branch grows where you don't want it. Fertilize lightly with all-purpose organic fertilizer once or twice a year. Pests and diseases show little interest in germander.

❀ *Cut it.* Germander is a nice, compact evergreen that makes a good wreath base and filler for dried and fresh arrangements. Its leaves complement any other colored flowers or plant material.

Ginger *Zingiber* spp.

❋ *Learn about it.* The name "ginger" covers a wide group of tropical plants including the culinary herb zingiber. All gingers are edible, but only species in the *Zingiber* genus really taste good. The rest are primarily ornamental, and they are indeed beautiful and fragrant. Ginger is a native of Asia and has figured in Chinese medicine for a long time. Marco Polo reported seeing huge plantations of ginger growing in China. It was once thought to protect against marauding tigers! (For another tiger repellant, see lemon grass on p. 84.)

It was brought to Europe by China traders and was quickly recognized as both medicinally and culinarily valuable. Some of the ornamental gingers hail from Australia. The Romans brought ginger to England where it was so popular it was set on wealthy tables along with salt and pepper to season most foods. It was expensive, though, and in the fourteenth century a pound of ginger cost the same as a whole sheep. Spaniards brought it to the New World, especially to Jamaica and South America where it could be grown as a cash crop and sent back to Europe by the shipload. The Portuguese established slave-tended fields in West Africa and Brazil, and ginger was quickly incorporated into African and slave cookery.

The most useful part of the plant is the rhizome that grows underground. These underground stems are called "hands." The fresh hands didn't hold up well when toted around the world on ships or caravans, though, so dried ginger became the spice of choice in many cultures. Now that ginger is available fresh all over the world, many cooks still use the dried form out of habit and tradition. Fresh ginger, however, is superior in flavor.

✹ *Grow it.* Because they are tropical or semi-tropical plants, gingers must be grown in warm climates or in containers that can be protected during the winter. Gingers are one of those groups of plants to which gardeners become easily addicted. That is because there are so many choices, we end up wanting them all. Some are tall; some are short. Some have big flowers; others have small exotic blooms. Some smell wonderful; others have little scent.

Generally, gingers prefer a shady or partially shady spot with rich soil. They like lots of organic material in the soil and a minimal amount of moisture. Plant them in the fall or spring in areas where the soil doesn't freeze or anytime if you are planting in a container. These are tough and vigorously growing plants. Put them in the ground and water until they are established. Mulch heavily in the winter and cut back the dead top in time for spring growth to begin. Most gingers bloom on one-year-old stems, but some will bloom the first year they are planted. Once culinary ginger is established, you can harvest pieces of root without digging up the whole plant. Just dig down and break off a piece of root to use, replace the disturbed soil, give your plant a drink of water, and it should keep growing without skipping a beat.

Common ginger produces less showy flowers than many of the other types, but it is still an interesting and lovely plant to grow. The leaves are lance-shaped, and the flowers are white with purple streaks. These are large plants, so give them room, probably at the back of the bed.

You can start your common ginger plant from a root from the grocery store. Pick a fat hand with several "fingers" and simply place it flat in the soil. (The sprouts will figure out which way is up.) The more beautiful ornamental varieties are available from specialty nurseries. Check around to see what is available in your neighborhood.

Most gingers are heavy feeders and like a rich soil. Feed them regularly with a good all-purpose organic plant food and enrich in-ground beds with lots of compost.

✲ *Eat it.* Gingersnaps, gingerbread, ginger beer, and ginger ale are just a few of the standard food products that get their zip from ginger. Ginger is a hot, spicy taste, and a little goes a long way. A fresh ginger root can be stored in the freezer in a plastic bag and removed to grate off whatever is needed. (Peel the section you plan to use before grating.) The remaining ginger should then be returned to the freezer where it will keep for a long time.

Ginger is a very versatile flavor. It makes delicious cold drinks, goes well with seafood and chicken, blends with fruit and vegetables, and can be crystallized into candy. It has a sweet, peppery warmth that seems to go with just about anything. To substitute fresh ginger in recipes that call for dried, use 1 tablespoon grated fresh root for ⅛ teaspoon dried ground ginger. Add grated ginger to salad dressings, applesauce, hamburger patties and anything else that you think could use a little zip.

✲ *Drink it.* To make ginger tea, peel and slice a 2-inch piece of ginger root. Add to a pan containing 4 cups boiling water. Cover and simmer for 15–20 minutes. Strain and serve. Add lemon and honey to taste. If the tea seems too strong to you, reduce simmering time or add more water. Some very nice commercial ginger teas are available.

Ginger and Lemon Tea: Boil 1 quart water and pour over 2 cups dried (or 4 cups fresh) lemon verbena leaves and ¼ cup freshly grated ginger. Let steep 20 minutes. Add juice of 1 lemon, ¼ cup honey. Strain and chill. Serve over ice with lemon or lime slices as garnish.

✲ *Cut it.* Some ginger flowers make gorgeous cut flowers and scent the room at the same time. Members of the *Curcuma* and *Hedychium* genuses are particularly lovely as ornamental plants with fragrant flowers in many different shapes and forms.

✱   *Soothe with it.* Ginger is best known as a stomach-calmer. The cake we know now as gingerbread began as a slice of bread wrapped around some ginger and served after a large dinner to calm the stomach. Eventually, the ginger was added to the bread before cooking and a little sweetener was added—voila! Gingerbread.

Ginger has shown the ability to stop nausea and dizziness in several clinical trials and is being investigated as an anti-inflammatory agent in the treatment of arthritis. A ginger tea is often used for every kind of stomach upset from morning sickness to travel sickness. If you like spicy food, you can chew a small piece of a root to deter travel sickness. The tea is also said to be good for flatulence, poor circulation, colds, and flu.

Gotu Kola *Centella asiatica*

❀ *Learn about it.* Gotu kola is native to the warmer regions of India, Asia, and Africa. It has been used for centuries as a medicinal herb by European, Indian, and Chinese herbalists. It is also said to be a favorite food of elephants—a handy piece of information in case you run upon a hungry elephant. Like most ancient herbs, gotu kola has many popular names. It has been called Asiatic pennywort, Indian pennywort, thickleaved pennywort, elephant plant, marshpenny, and mandookaparni.

❀ *Grow it.* Gotu kola makes an excellent ground cover or hanging basket plant. It grows by sending out baby plants from the mother plant, sort of like ajuga or strawberries. You can start it from seed or by taking a cutting from a neighbor's plant. Native to hot, damp areas, gotu kola requires additional water and appreciates shade from the hot sun. The leaves are small and rounded and light green and very attractive on a shady porch or around the house. If you plant it in the ground, make sure it has room to roam since it will spread quickly, much like mint.

❀ *Eat it.* You can use gotu kola leaves as a salad by themselves, combined with onion or shallot and dressed with lime or lemon juice, or combine it with other greens for a healthy treat.

✺ *Drink it.* This herb is often found in Asian markets where you may also find a bright green pennywort drink that is thirst quenching and delicious in spite of its slightly repelling color. You can also make your own.

Gotu Kola Drink: Remove stems from a handful of gotu kola leaves and wash well. Add 2½ cups cold water and ½ cup simple syrup. (Make syrup by combining equal parts sugar and water and boiling to dissolve sugar. Cool and store in refrigerator. You can use this in many drinks, including the ever-popular Mint Julep.) Add 3–4 ice cubes and blend at high speed until everything is well mixed and chopped. Serve immediately or it will turn an icky shade of green.

✺ *Soothe with it.* When gotu kola was introduced into the United States herbal world a few years ago, there seemed to be nothing this plant couldn't do. It was said to heal wounds, increase circulation, enhance memory, increase vitality, cure skin disorders, act as an aphrodisiac, enhance the immune system, and on and on. Maybe so. We *do* know it contains vitamins A, D, E, K, C, B1, B2, B3, B5, B6, B9, B12, choline, inositol, vitamin H, and a long list of amino acids. It also contains calcium, chloride, magnesium, phosphorus, potassium, sodium and sulfur plus trace elements of many other minerals.

Even in the highly skeptical pharmaceutical world, gotu kola is used to make an extract that is then combined with other chemicals to make a wide range of products including slimming formulas, firming products, wound healing products, anti-aging skin creams, and more.

The main benefit of gotu kola seems to be as a general tonic. It stimulates blood flow and cleansing. It is said to keep people young and full of energy. It also serves as a mild diuretic. It tastes a lot like parsley, one of its close relatives. It has also been used topically to treat wounds, either in a poultice or with just a leaf placed on small cuts and scratches.

Horehound *Marrubium vulgare*

✺ *Learn about it.* There are two plants known as horehound. White horehound (*Marrubium vulgare*), commonly known simply as horehound, is the one most often grown as a garden plant and the only one that can be taken internally except under directions of a professional. Black horehound (*Billola nigra*), also known as black stinking horehound, is an unpleasant smelling, weedy plant with limited use.

White horehound is native to Britain, where it has grown for a long time in cottage gardens. It is traditionally made into tea and candy and is also made into horehound ale in Norfolk and other areas of England where it is very popular. Romans used it for its medicinal properties, and Egyptians believe it could serve as an antidote to poisons.

✺ *Grow it.* Horehound is a perennial plant that is easy to grow and flourishes in dry, poor soil. It needs full sun and has a sort of weedy appearance, but I prefer to think of it as "casual." Bees love the flowers, which do not appear until the second year of growth. The foliage is gray-green and flowers are white. It grows easily from seed or from division. (To divide a plant, dig up an existing clump, then gently separate the roots into individual plants. If the roots are intertwined, cut them with a sharp knife to create new plants.) To keep the growing and expanding plant from getting out of hand, cut off the flowers once they start to produce seed.

Planted near tomatoes and peppers, horehound stimulates growth and aids in the fruiting of those plants.

☀ *Attract with it.* The small flowers are attractive to Tachnid and Syrid flies and Braconid and Icheumonid wasps. In the larval stage, these beneficial insects parasitize or eat many insect pests. The plant blooms over a long period of time, so it keeps attracting beneficials to your garden. All kinds of bees love it.

☀ *Deter with it.* An infusion of horehound sprayed on fruit trees will help kill cankerworm, and an infusion of horehound in milk left in a dish is said to kill any flies that come around.

☀ *Soothe with it.* Horehound is a very bitter herb. But, a tea of horehound drunk cold is said to ease digestion and heartburn and also to destroy intestinal worms. At the first sign of a cold, some people chop 9 small leaves and mix them with 1 tablespoon honey, then eat slowly to ease sore throat or cough, repeating as necessary.

☀ *Stop coughing with it.* The best known use of horehound is as a cough suppressant and expectorant. Children used to be given horehound candy to treat a cough, and some even came to think it tasted good! Add enough sugar to anything and someone will like it! Horehound Candy: Combine 4 ounces fresh horehound leaves, 1 teaspoon crushed anise seed, 3 crushed cardamom seeds, and 2½ cups water. Simmer for 20 minutes and strain through a fine filter. Over low heat, dissolve 2 cups white sugar and 1½ cups brown sugar in the herb liquid. Boil over medium heat to the hard ball stage. Pour onto buttered cooking sheet. Score while still warm and break into small pieces when cool. Store candy in waxed paper and suck as needed for cough.

Horseradish *Armoracia rusticana*

✻ *Learn about it.* A native of Europe, horseradish, like most herbs, was first known as a medicinal plant and only later came to be used as a flavoring. Although both root and leaf are used, the root is the most powerful part of the plant and is widely used for many purposes.

The Germans and Danes began using horseradish to create a pungent fish sauce in the 1500s. Once it spread to Britain in the 1600s, it became associated with beef, a combination we continue today.

✻ *Grow it.* Horseradish is easy to grow and can become invasive. It is a hardy perennial plant. Be sure to plant it where it has room to grow or put it in a large container. You can also use the bottomless pot method to keep it from taking over. Plant it in full sun in rich, loose soil with good drainage. Since the root is the part you want to use, give it good soil to encourage good growth. You also need loose soil so you can get to a side root to detach it from the main plant when you are ready to use it.

Since the root is the part of the plant most used, you will want to dig a piece of root in the spring or fall to use. You can divide the plant in the winter and share with friends or reduce your clump by putting some into the compost heap. Fall roots have a stronger flavor than spring roots.

✻ *Eat it.* Horseradish is a pungent herb with plenty of flavor in the volatile oils that reside in the plant. These all dissipate, however, on cooking, so use horseradish raw. The young leaves can be added to salads for a spicy zip, but it is the root that cooks (and diners) love.

Find a plump root and wash it thoroughly, then dry. You can slice it and dry it for later use, but most people make it into sauce right away. Horseradish Sauce: Grind with vinegar and salt in blender or food processor, adjusting amounts depending on size of root. Store in a sterilized jar in the refrigerator. It will keep for a long time and can be used as is or added to sour cream or other milder flavored ingredients to make a variety of sauces. It is traditionally used in red seafood sauce and white sauce for beef. Grate the root directly into coleslaw, dips, pickled beets, cream cheese, mayonnaise, and avocado. Use sparingly.

For some reason, horseradish is stronger when it is cold than when it is at room temperature, so keep that in mind when you are using it. Taste as you go to get just the right amount of flavor.

✺ *Deter with it.* Plant small roots in containers around potatoes to repel Colorado potato bug and improve disease resistance. Horseradish also helps repel blister beetles, an unpleasant little stinging bug that gets on tomatoes and other garden plants and defoliates them.

A horseradish infusion can be used as a preventative for fungal diseases in plants. It is especially helpful with brown rot in apple trees. Process 1 cup of root in food processor until finely chopped. Combine this with 16 ounces water in glass container and let soak for 24 hours. Strain, compost the solids, and mix the liquid with 2 quarts of water and spray.

✺ *Get pretty with it.* It is said that slicing horseradish and letting it sit in milk for a while will create a lotion that improves skin clarity. Keep in the refrigerator.

✺ *Stay healthy with it.* Horseradish roots contain significant amounts of calcium, sodium, magnesium, and vitamin C. It is a powerful circulatory stimulant, and a poultice made of chopped horseradish root has been used to ease the aches and pains in joints and muscles by sending blood to the hurting places.

The root has antibiotic qualities that are said to be useful for protecting the intestinal tract. A healthy bite of horseradish will also bring an immediate clearing of the sinuses.

✺ *Treat Fido with it.* Adding finely chopped horseradish leaves to dog food is said to help dogs expel any intestinal worms. It also improves their general health and body tone.

Lavender *Lavandula officinalis*

❋ *Learn about it.* Lavender has been in use for at least 2,500 years. The name comes from the Latin meaning "to wash." In the King James Version of the Bible, it is called by the name "spikenard." It was used by Egyptians, Phoenicians, and the peoples of Arabia as a perfume and as part of the ritual embalming process. In the days when the world was a smelly place, plants with sweet and potent scents were treasured. Roman men and women anointed themselves heavily with a strong scent of lavender. In the first century, Greek naturalist Pedanius Dioscorides praised the medicinal attributes of lavender. Roman legend said that poisonous vipers made their nests in lavender bushes. This belief drove up the price of lavender and may have been started by those who had it growing on their property!

The history of lavender spans the globe, with its use by royals and other distinguished people both as a fragrance and as a guard against disease. It was one of the herbs believed to ward off the Plague during those horrible years. Cleopatra, the Queen of Sheba, and Judith (in the book of the Apocrypha bearing her name) all used lavender to seduce their important lovers.

❋ *Grow it.* Deciding which kind of lavender to grow can be a challenge. There are many different varieties, each with slightly different flower forms and plant habits. Some are more cold-hardy than others; some have longer bloom periods. The best way to find a variety that you like is to visit a nursery that has several plants from which to choose. Sniff and look and see what appeals to you. Growing lavender from seed is usually disappointing, so find a good source of small plants and start your lavender garden there. Select several types and see which one does best in your garden.

Lavender requires full sun and perfect drainage. It prefers rocky soil and low humidity. In some areas with high humidity, growing lavender as an annual is the only option. You can try mulching with small pebbles to keep the plant dry and watering infrequently on the ground rather than on the foliage. Plant your young plants at the level they were growing or slightly lower and water well. Do not water again until the soil is dry. Feed sparingly with an all-purpose organic fertilizer. Harvest the flowers as they mature. Both the leaves and flowers are fragrant.

✦ *Sniff it.* The greatest charm of lavender is its fragrance. You can enjoy that fragrance in a variety of ways. Fresh lavender cut and brought into the house makes a lovely arrangement. Dried lavender keeps its scent for a long time. You can burn the stems like incense to spread the nice smell throughout a room. Just passing through the garden when lavender is in bloom is a treat. Visiting a lavender farm can be intoxicating.

✦ *Cook with it.* Use lavender in the kitchen. There are lots of delightful recipes that use lavender in sweet and savory dishes.

✦ *Drink it.* Using dried or fresh lavender flowers, make a tea by pouring 1 cup boiling water over 1–2 teaspoons flowers and letting steep 5–10 minutes. Strain and serve.

Lavender Margaritas: Blend 1 cup tequila, ⅓ cup Triple Sec, 1 cup canned coconut milk, and ¼ cup limeade concentrate. Blend on high speed, then gradually add 2 cups frozen unsweetened raspberries, 2 cups frozen unsweetened blueberries, 2 teaspoons dried lavender buds, and 4 ice cubes. Whirl until smooth and slushy. Pour into glasses. Add lavender sprig for garnish.

Lavender Lemonade: Boil 2½ cups of water with 1½ cups sugar. Add 12 stems of fresh lavender and remove the pan from the heat. Place the lid on and let cool. When cool, add 2½ cups of water and 2¼ cups lemon juice. Strain out the lavender and serve over crushed ice. Garnish with lavender blossoms.

★ *Sweeten it up.* Combine lavender flowers with honey or sugar and use to sweeten tea, lemonade, or other beverages. Use a mortar and pestle to grind the flowers into a fine dust. You can also use the lavender sugar in recipes for cookies, pound cake, or other sweets that call for plain sugar.

★ *Make vinegar with it.* Pack lavender stems, leaves, and flowers in a quart jar, then fill with white vinegar. Let it sit for several days, shaking occasionally. When vinegar smells like lavender, strain out the plant material and pour the vinegar into a bottle. Use the vinegar as a rinse for dark hair or as a cleaning preparation in your kitchen or bathroom.

★ *Freshen with it.* Use lavender water as a refreshing cologne, to scent linens, and as an astringent facial splash. Its antiseptic qualities are good for treating and preventing facial acne. Lavender Water: In very clean container with a lid, place 1½ cups lavender flower. Pour in 2 cups distilled water. Add ¼ cup vodka. Put the lid on the container and shake until everything is well mixed. Put in a sunny spot for 2 weeks. Strain through a coffee filter and store the remaining lavender water in the refrigerator. The alcohol kills any bacteria and prolongs the scent. You can also spray lavender water lightly on your linens to give them a nice fresh scent.

Infusion of lavender makes good hair rinses, bath additions, or air freshener.

★ *Package it.* Combine dried lavender flowers and leaves in a small pillow and use the sachet to scent drawers and closets. The sachets will also repel moths in your closet or drawers. The wonderful scent will please you but will drive away insect pests. You can also make dream pillows to put under your regular pillow to create lovely scents and sweet dreams while you sleep.

★ *Make a potpourri.* Combine lavender with other dried flowers and plants to create room freshening bowls of fragrance. Use any potpourri recipe and add lots of lavender to the mix.

★ *Soothe with it.* Soaking a cloth in lavender water and lying down with it across the forehead may help relax tension, relieve stress, and ease headaches. Lavender tea is also said to calm nerves, headaches, and flatulence.

Lemon Balm *Melissa officinalis*

Victor Z. Martin 2007

✸ *Learn about it.* Lemon balm was used as a medicine by the Greeks more than two thousand years ago. It was called "heart's delight" in Southern Europe because it was said to dispel melancholy and depression. A fragrant and tasty herb, it has been put to many uses throughout the years and is still a favorite garden plant.

✸ *Grow it.* Lemon balm literally grows like a weed. It is best known for its rapid growth and tendency to take over the spot where it is growing—and the spot next to that. It will be happy in full sun or partial shade, has no particular soil requirements, and needs only moderate amounts of water. If it begins to look ragged, simply cut the plant to the ground and it will send out new lovely leaves. There are green and variegated varieties to choose from. If you don't want a lot of lemon balm, try growing it in a container. It is a lovely plant in high shade, perhaps on a patio or porch, and will drape nicely over the edges of the container.

✸ *Eat it.* Use finely chopped leaves in salads, sauces for fish, mayonnaise, sauerkraut, fruit salads, drinks, or jellies. You can make a tea of lemon balm or add it to your regular tea. Good iced or hot, lemon balm tea has a gentle lemony-mint flavor. Use only fresh leaves or tea. Cooked leaves look and taste yucky. It also makes a nice garnish for cold drinks and salads in the summer.

🐢 *Attract with it.* Bees love the fragrance and insignificant flowers of lemon balm.

🐢 *Deter with it.* Lemon balm contains citronella compounds, so dried crushed leaves deter many pests. You can rub it on your skin to repel mosquitoes and sprinkle it on the ground in the garden to repel squash bugs.

🐢 *Dry it.* The nice lemony scent remains when the leaves are dried. Add it to potpourri or dried arrangements and enjoy it year-round.

🐢 *Freshen with it.* Add a strong infusion of lemon balm to furniture polish or to your bath water. Add it to vinegar to improve the scent when you are cleaning.

🐢 *Soothe with it.* Crushed leaves or a poultice of lemon balm has been used on insect bites or sores on the skin to help soothe the hurt and encourage healing. Some people drink hot tea of lemon balm to ease bronchitis, colds, headaches, and calm and uplift spirits. It is also said to promote long life.

Lemon Grass *Cymbopogon citratus*

❋ *Learn about it.* Lemon grass is native to Asia and Australia. It has been used in the cuisines of Asia, India, and the Caribbean. Lemon grass has been used for centuries in Indonesia and Malaysia by herbalists and in Ayurvedic herbalism. It is grown commercially in India and Asia today to be used in perfume, soap, insect repellants, aromatherapy products, and candles.

❋ *Grow it.* A tropical plant, lemon grass needs a warm climate in which to thrive. Plant it in a sunny spot with good soil and protect it from cold and winds. It makes a nice grassy clumping plant about 3 feet tall with leaves that move gracefully in the breeze. You can also grow lemon grass in a large container, making it easier to protect in the winter. It is a perennial that will die to the ground in the winter and come back in the spring if it doesn't get too cold. Protect the roots in winter with heavy mulching or dig a portion of the plant to put into a pot and bring indoors until spring arrives. In either case, cut back the top before cold weather settles in. Be sure to mark its location if you leave it in the ground so you won't mistake it for Johnson grass when it comes up in the spring.

Unlike other grasses used as ornamentals in the garden, lemon grass does not have a large seed head. Although it does bloom in its native lands, it rarely blooms here.

Be careful when working with lemon grass because the edges of the leaves are sharp. It is said that in India, lemon grass is planted around homes to keep tigers away—it hurts their little paws!

✦ *Eat it.* The most intense flavor in the lemon grass plant is in the white fleshy base of the leaves that grows right next to the root. This is a very fibrous part of the plant and should not actually be eaten, but it is great for flavoring. Chop or crush the base of the leaf and cook it in stock or water to extract the flavor. Discard the plant and use the liquid for flavoring. You can also finely chop the leaves to add to recipes.

The rising interest in lemon grass in the United States coincided with the growing interest in cuisine from Southeast Asia, particularly Vietnamese and Thai dishes. This herb has a nice lemony flavor without the sharp-sourness of lemon. The flavor combines well with garlic, hot chile peppers, and other flavors standard in those cooking traditions. Coincidentally, those flavors are also standard in cuisine of Mexico and the Southwest.

Lemon Grass Salsa: Combine 2 stalks lemon grass (including leaves) smashed and cut into large pieces, 2 medium sized tomatoes chopped, 1 chile pepper (with heat to suit your taste) chopped, 1 small onion diced, 1 garlic clove pressed, 2 tablespoons chopped cilantro, 2 table-spoons olive oil, 2 tablespoons red wine vinegar, salt to taste. Let the mixture sit for about an hour at room temperature. Remove lemon grass, stir well, and serve or refrigerate for later use.

✦ *Drink it.* Lemon Grass Tea: Add ¼ cup chopped lemon grass leaves to 4 cups boiling water. Steep for 8–10 minutes, strain, and serve over ice. Sweeten to taste.

✦ *Deter with it.* Crush the white fleshy base of a leaf of lemon grass and rub the juice on your exposed body parts to help keep away mosquitoes. The plant is grown commercially to make mosquito repellant, but you can make your own on the spot with just a little hand smashing. You can also make a tincture of lemon grass by combining 5–6 stalk bases chopped and put into a blender with 1 cup vodka. Blend and strain. Add ½ cup water and put into spray bottle. Mist yourself, kids, and pets with this concoction to keep away mosquitoes.

Victor Z. Martino
2006

Lemon Verbena *Aloysia triphylla*

✹   *Learn about it.* A native of Chile, lemon verbena was brought to Europe by the Spanish in the 1700s. They loved its perfume, and it was first used only as a fragrant herb. Because lemons were rare commodities in Europe, lemon verbena was prized as a substitute. It returned to the New World with missionaries and settlers and spread across the continent.

✹   *Grow it.* Lemon verbena makes a nice informal shrub with bright green leaves and woody stems. The bush sort of rambles off in different directions and is not compact, but it is wonderfully adaptable and can easily be trimmed to keep it roughly in the shape you want it. It is easy to grow, is of no interest to most pests, does not need a lot of fertilizer, and grows quickly.

Plant in full sun in good garden soil. Because it gets tall and rangy, plant it at the back of a bed or in a line of shrubs. Keep moist until established, it then quickly becomes drought-tolerant and requires little or no attention.

The leaves will all fall off when winter comes, but lemon verbena is one of the first plants to leaf out in the spring. Its spray of pale flowers in the spring isn't impressive but is fragrant and sweet. In a perennial border, lemon verbena is a great companion to evergreen plants like rosemary.

✹   *Substitute it for lemons.* If you have no lemons in the fridge when you start dinner, go outside and clip some lemon verbena leaves instead. Its crisp, clean lemon taste makes it a perfect substitute in any recipe that calls for lemons. Use fresh leaves and chop them to add to your other ingredients. The amount of lemon verbena you use will depend on how lemony you want your dish to be.

🌸   *Make jelly out of it.* When you cut off errant branches that are taking up too much space in the garden, make a strong tea of the leaves and use that juice to make jelly. Lemon verbena jelly is fragrant and has a nice fresh taste that is good with breakfast or with meats and other main course dishes. It is wonderful in shortbread cookies that call for a jelly filling.

🌸   *Drink it.* Make tea with it and drink it by itself or add to regular tea or lemonade. It is good both cold and hot.

Spiced Tea: 2 cups dried lemon verbena leaves, 1 cup dried orange peel, 1 cup dried chamomile flowers, 3 tablespoons whole cloves crushed, 1 cup dried orange mint, 1 6-inch cinnamon stick crushed. Blend all ingredients and store in covered container. When ready to use, shake container and spoon 1 teaspoon tea into pot for each cup of tea that you want. Add boiling water and steep 5–10 minutes. Strain and serve. Sweeten with honey if you wish.

🌸   *Dry it.* To be sure you have enough lemon flavor to last through the winter, dry leaves of lemon verbena either by hanging them in a dry spot out of the sun or by wrapping them in paper towels and microwaving them on low until the leaves are dry and crisp. Put them in an airtight container and use them throughout the cold season.

🌸   *Soothe with it.* A cup of tea has mild sedative properties, so some people drink a cup at bed time to help encourage a good night's sleep. It is also said to be good for bronchial or nasal congestion and indigestion. Note: Tea made from lemon verbena should be drunk in moderation.

🌸   *Sniff it.* Herb pillows, sachets, and sofa sacks stuffed with dried lemon verbena leaves will all add fragrance to your home. The fresh lemony scent is welcome in any room and never becomes overly sweet or cloying. Just crush the dried leaves and stuff them into whatever size pillow you desire. Every time you punch the pillow you will release the heavenly scent.

Victor Z. Martin
2005

Marigold *Tagetes* spp.

There are several useful types of marigold with different looks, histories, and characteristics. The common garden marigolds are generally African or French marigolds (both of which come from Mexico). They are wonderful garden plants, but I am concentrating here on the herbal members of the clan:

Mexican Mint Marigold
Tagetes lucida

✸ *Learn about it.* Also known as simply mint marigold as well as Texas tarragon, Spanish tarragon, sweet mace, and yerba anise, this plant comes from Central America. In Mexico and Guatemala where it grows wild, the leaves have been used as teas, seasoning, and medicine for at least a thousand years. The Aztecs used it as a medicinal herb and in rituals, and it was exported to Europe in the 1800s. The Europeans then brought it back to the New World with the name "false tarragon."

Texas is so proud of it that a legislator suggested it be named the official state herb. So far, nothing is official.

✸ *Grow it.* In addition to being a useful herb, mint marigold is a lovely perennial landscape plant. It is easy to grow in well-drained soil. It can take full sun or partial shade and grows to 2–3 feet tall, making a nice low hedge. It dies down in the winter but comes back strong every year with little care or attention. The yellow flowers cheer up a sometimes dreary garden by blooming in the late summer or early fall.

★ *Eat it.* Both the flowers and the leaves of the Mexican mint marigold are edible and can be used year-round if dried.

★ *Season with it.* Mexican mint marigold is sometimes marketed as Texas tarragon because its nice mild licorice flavor is very much like that of French tarragon, which really doesn't like high summer heat. So, when you find a recipe that calls for tarragon, use mint marigold instead. It is a direct substitute—1 tsp for 1 tsp.

Use it in herbal butters, salad dressings, with chicken (a favorite for those who love tarragon chicken or tarragon chicken salad), and many other dishes.

★ *Garnish with it.* The yellow flowers of late summer or early fall are perfect garnishes for any dish. You can use them in salads, on serving platters, or in drinks.

★ *Drink it.* You can make a hot or iced tea from Mexican mint marigold by itself or add the herb to regular iced tea for a rootbeer or sarsaparilla flavor.

★ *Make vinegar with it.* One of the most popular herbal vinegars around is tarragon vinegar. Mexican mint marigold is a great substitute for tarragon in vinegar as well as other recipes. Place a bunch of leaves in a jar and fill with your favorite vinegar. Let it sit for a couple of weeks, then strain out the plant material and pour the vinegar into an attractive bottle. Use in salads and recipes. If you are making your vinegar while the plant is in flower, add some blossoms to the vinegar for color and taste.

★ *Cut it.* This nice herb blooms cheerfully in a burst of bright yellow flowers. They are wonderful to cut and use in the house in bouquets. They look perky and smell great.

★ *Dry it.* You can dry it in the fall before the plant freezes by using any of a number of methods. Hang a bunch to dry in a draft-free location with good ventilation and no direct sun. Or, place leaves and flowers without stems between sheets of paper towels and dry in the microwave.

Go slow until you find the right length of time that dries but does not desiccate the plant. You want it bright green and dry. (This makes the house smell wonderful!) Another alternative is to use a dehydrator and follow manufacturer's suggestions. The flowers retain their color when dried, and the flowers and leaves retain their scent, so Mexican mint marigold is a perfect addition to potpourris and herbal wreaths.

✺   *Soothe with it.* Mexican mint marigold tea is said to soothe an upset stomach and is often used in Mexico for that purpose.

Lemon Marigold *Tagetes lemmonii*

✺   *Learn about it.* So, you figure it is named *lemmonii* because it smells like lemons, right? Wrong! This plant was found growing in Arizona in the 1800s by a couple of plant collectors named Lemmon. Thus the name. The Lemmons took the plant with them to California and established it there and sent some plants to England where it became popular. It was used as a medicinal plant in Mexico, and apparently the Spanish missionaries who found it there also made it a part of their medicinal supplies.

Another common name is Copper Canyon daisy, and you are right if you guess it got that name because it grows wild in the Copper Canyon region of Mexico.

✺   *Grow it.* Lemon marigold is one of those plants that people either love or hate. The smell is very pronounced and as much like camphor as it is like lemon, but no one disputes that it is strong. It is easy to grow in full sun with good drainage. It will make a sprawling plant that can take severe pruning when it gets out of hand. Its gray-green, finely cut leaves make a nice foil for other plants. The plant is drought-tolerant and very low-maintenance. It thrives on high heat and will do well in intensely hot areas facing west, against a brick wall, or surrounded by concrete. It will die back in the winter only to emerge in the spring ready to go again. Trimming back in late fall or early winter will get your plant off to a good start.

The bright yellow flowers of lemon marigold bloom in spring and fall. It reacts to day length and chooses its bloom-time accordingly.

✶ *Attract with it.* Bees and butterflies like the sharp fragrance and bright flowers of the lemon marigold plant. Birds like it too, as do most people.

✶ *Deter with it.* Well, there are always those people who don't like it, but lemon marigold also repels deer. This is one of the few plants that deer really do not like and generally will not eat unless they are absolutely starving. Whiteflies and other common garden insect pests are repelled by the strong scent as well.

✶ *Cut it.* If you enjoy the scent, lemon marigolds make dandy cut flowers. They will fill a room with their fragrance and brighten up any corner. They also add their special scent to potpourri.

Victor Z Martin
2007

Mint *Mentha* spp.

✹ *Learn about it.* Mint has traditionally been known as the herb of hospitality and fun. It has a fresh, lively taste that is bound to cheer you up—whether you find it in Doublemint Gum or Mint Julep. Greeks and Romans used to crown themselves with peppermint at their parties and used the herb as table decorations as well as for flavoring food, sauces, and wines.

There are more than six hundred varieties of mint (and counting), and all but pennyroyal can be eaten freely. In the Bible, mint was even accepted as payment to the temple. Because it is so easily grown, its restorative and refreshing qualities have been enjoyed for centuries by people of all stations of life. In fact, it grows wild in almost every country where it has been introduced as a garden plant. It was grown in convent gardens in the ninth century, and Geoffrey Chaucer mentioned it in his writing. The Pilgrims brought spearmint to the New World. It is mentioned in the Icelandic Pharmacopoeias of the thirteenth century.

The name "mint" comes from Greek mythology. Menthe was a nymph who had the misfortune of having Pluto fall in love with her. His jealous wife, Proserpine, turned her into a plant.

One name for mint in Spanish is *yerba buena*—the good herb—because it is healthy as well as flavorful. This was also the original name the early Spanish settlers gave to what is now San Francisco. More pious Spaniards came along later and changed the name to honor St. Francis.

Peppermint and spearmint are the most common types of mint, but there are also many others that are grown in gardens around the world, especially apple, chocolate, lemon, basil, pineapple, ginger, and pennyroyal. A large industry is involved in distilling the oils of various mints to be used medicinally and as flavoring for food.

✹   *Grow it.* Mint is easy to grow, regardless of the variety. It is a low-growing, creeping plant that can spread all over the garden if given any encouragement. The stems root as they travel across the soil, so it is easy to get a transplant from a friend or neighbor. If there are no roots on the clipping, the plant also roots easily in water or soil.

Although traditional wisdom says to grow mint in the shade, its essential oils are stronger when it grows in the sun. Mint will grow under almost any conditions as long as it has ample water. It grows in sun or shade, rich or poor soil. Do not try to grow it from seed, however. The seeds are unreliable and you will be disappointed in the results.

Plant your mint in a space where it has room to grow, or put it in a container if you don't want it to spread. It makes an excellent ground cover under shrubbery, roses, or other taller plants. If it grows out into the lawn, it smells great when it is run over with the lawnmower. Pennyroyal is also an excellent groundcover since it is very low-growing.

Keep new plants watered until they are established. Once they are growing, they become more drought-tolerant. A liberal top dressing of compost in the spring will help them grow steadily. Cut down the spindly stems when they begin to look ragged, and the plants will quickly regenerate themselves. In warm climates, mint is evergreen and looks good throughout the year.

About the only disease that attacks mint is rust. If you have rust in your garden, pull up the mint and throw it away and plant some more in a container. You can't treat the plants in the ground successfully.

Otherwise, mint is a carefree garden plant that smells good, looks good, and tastes good.

✹   *Eat it.* Don't eat pennyroyal, but do eat all the rest of the mints. Peppermint's volatile oil, which contains menthol, is used commercially to flavor medicine, candies, liqueurs, cigarettes, and all sorts of other things. Peppermint flavoring is one of the most universal tastes around and for good reason. It is bright and cheerful and tastes good.

Spearmint is a little less strong, but it is also used widely as flavoring in mint sauce, jelly, gum, candy, liqueurs, and baked goods. Most people look for the mint that they knew in their childhood—what they think of as "regular mint." Most often that is spearmint.

Mints are excellent additions to salads, especially fruit salads, and are traditionally served with peas and other spring vegetables. Chop chocolate mint and add it to your favorite chocolate cake or brownie recipe. It is also good chopped up into hot cocoa.

Mint Relish: Grate the rind of one orange into a bowl. Peel and chop the orange into the same bowl. Add 1 cup applesauce and ½ cup fresh mint leaves, chopped. Stir well and refrigerate for several hours before serving. Good with any dinner—meat or vegetable.

❀ *Drink it.* No drinks are more traditional in the South than ones flavored with mint. A wonderful refreshing drink for summer can be made by simply adding sprigs of fresh mint to a pitcher or carafe of water. Let it sit a little while and serve over ice. Or, fill a sun tea jar with ice and water, add mint, and put it on the counter to sip from all day. Add ice as it melts. You can also make a hot tea of any mint leaf. Simply steep in boiling water for about 5 minutes and sweeten to taste.

And of course, it would be impossible to run the Kentucky Derby without Mint Juleps: Place 1 teaspoon water and 1 teaspoon sugar and 5–6 fresh mint leaves in a tumbler (preferably one made of sterling silver). Mash with a spoon until the sugar is dissolved and the mint releases its scent. Fill the glass with crushed ice. Slowly pour in 2 ounces of good Bourbon whiskey. Stir gently and decorate with a sprig of mint. Sit back and enjoy the race—or just enjoy the drink.

❀ *Cut it.* There is really no reason to use dried mint in temperate climates. You can snip fresh mint anytime and it always tastes better, but if you want to dry it, you can easily do so in the microwave. Wrap sprigs of mint in paper towels and microwave in short spurts until the leaves are dry but still nice and green. Store in a dark, dry spot. The added benefit of this method is that it makes the kitchen smell divine.

✻ *Attract with it.* The menthol in mint is very attractive to beneficial insects. In addition, earthworms like mint plantings, and earthworms are a gardener's best friend.

✻ *Deter with it.* All mints act as a repellant for ants and other insects. If you have ants coming into your home, lay a sprig of mint in their path and it will turn them around and send them back outside. Pennyroyal planted outside your door is also said to keep out ants. You might want to try planting it around your outside air-conditioning unit to keep the fire ants away.

You can also make an all-purpose flea repellant pillow for any pet by stuffing a pillow with 1 cup fresh thyme, 2 cups fresh spearmint, and 1 cup fresh wormwood. Tuck it in your pet's bed or wherever the pet is inclined to recline. It will smell nice as it does its repelling. Note: Pennyroyal is also a good flea repellant, but it may be toxic for cats.

Mint planted beneath roses in the garden repels aphids. It also deters white cabbage moths, ants, rodents, flea beetles, fleas, aphids, and other pests wherever it is planted.

✻ *Soothe with it.* Peppermint is the strongest of the mints, but all contain menthol, which has been widely used in medicines. Some people drink peppermint tea to soothe an upset stomach and spearmint tea to improve a cold. In addition, menthol contains properties that are aromatic, antiseptic, calmative, antispasmodic, anti-inflammatory, antibacterial, anti-parasitic, and act as a stimulant. Using a macerated handful of mint leaves in oil for massage is said to be good for headaches and sore, aching muscles. Mint was first associated as an accompaniment to lamb because it was thought to help the body digest the immature meat. The combination of lamb and mint flavors have continued in use because they taste so good together.

Victor Z Martin
2007

Mullein *Verbascum nigrum*

★ *Learn about it.* In ancient Greek literature, mullein was given to Odysseus to protect him from the sorcery of Circe, who had already turned his crew into pigs. Now that is a useful herb!

Mullein has a long history of use as a magical protector against witchcraft and evil spirits. The belief that herbs have magic powers can often be traced to their use as medicinal herbs. After all, the ability to restore health could be considered pretty magical. Mullein was used by the Greeks in ancient times, the French during the Middle Ages, and everyone else since then.

Its common names are hag's taper, candlewick, flannel leaf, old man's flannel, flannel flower, velvet dock, and velvet plant. All the names refer to characteristics of the plant and its various uses.

★ *Grow it.* Mullein is a biennial that produces big velvety leaves with fine hairs the first year and tall stalks of little yellow flowers the second year. Mullein is easy to grow. You can start it from seed or transplants if you can find them. The plants reseed easily once established, which accounts for it growing wild in many parts of the country. It has nice grayish green leaves that are attractive in containers as well as in the garden. It can take heat and humidity and prospers with little care. Poor soil and minimal water are also no problem. Plant in sun or part shade in early spring and enjoy the large rosette of leaves that will quickly appear.

Mullein is a large plant so leave room for it to grow or put it in a large container. The rosette can reach a couple of feet in diameter, and the stalk can grow to 6–8 feet in height.

✻   *Attract with it.* Bees love mullein flowers. Plant some every year so that you always have a plant in bloom.

✻   *Dry it.* The leaves and flowers of mullein can be dried easily by hanging the plant in an airy, dry spot. Do not dry them with artificial heat, and be sure to remove the green part of the yellow flowers before drying them on a screen. The flowers are a good addition to potpourri because they maintain their color after they are dried.

✻   *Brighten up with it.* Traditionally, the stalks of the mullein plant were dipped in fat or tallow to form long-lasting iridescent torches. If you have a bunch, this would make unusual outdoor decorations for a party. On the other hand, you can brighten fair hair by rinsing it with an infusion of mullein flowers.

✻   *Soothe with it.* The root, leaves, and flowers of the mullein plant have all been used as folk medicines. A tea made of leaves (strained well through cheesecloth or a coffee filter to remove hairs from the leaves) is said to be useful in soothing sore throats and coughs. It combines expectorant action with soothing mucilage to help clear up congestion. A tincture of mullein has been used traditionally as a treatment for allergies. It is often taken to ward off seasonal allergies before they commence.

Mullein root has been used to support urinary tract health and help with bladder control. It also has been an ingredient in cough syrups and as a remedy for muscle spasms. The root is most commonly used in a tincture.

Native Americans made tea of mullein and also smoked the dried leaves to treat chest congestion. They also inhaled the steam rising from the tea to soothe the throat.

Steam from a tea of mullein flowers is said to be good for skin, too. (After pouring boiling water over a bowl or basin containing flowers, the person holds his or her head over the basin with a towel draped over to make a tent so the steam will sink into the pores.) Mixing the flowers into a bland cream can help smooth rough or dry skin. A tincture of the flowers has a mild sedative effect, helping some people sleep at night. Others soak flowers in olive oil for several days then use the oil as eardrops for an earache or to rub on aching joints to ease the pain.

A mixture of crushed, dried leaves mixed with ointment is thought to make a good treatment for skin ailments. It seems to have a drawing effect, quickly bringing boils, pimples, and other infected sores to a head so that they can heal.

Oregano *Origanum* spp.

✦ *Learn about it.* The name comes from the Greek and means "joy of the mountain." Oregano is native to the Mediterranean area and grows wild, as you might expect, in the mountainous regions. Oregano and marjoram are herbs that share similar tastes and characteristics and are often confused. In addition, there are "oreganos" that are not really oregano at all (Mexican oregano, for example.) They share many character- istics but cannot always be interchanged in recipes.

The Greeks believed that oregano had the power to banish sadness so it was often used in wedding ceremonies. In China, oregano has been used for centuries as a medicinal herb. Oregano was generally unknown and unused in the United States until soldiers who had served in Italy during WWII came home with a hankering for pizza.

✦ *Grow it.* Oregano thrives on poor soil, dry conditions, and friendly neglect. Its only serious requirement is good drainage. It can't tolerate wet feet. All prefer full sun but will take high shade. Like mint, oregano's flavor is stronger when it grows in the sun.

Low-growing oreganos will grow happily in a pot or hanging basket. Trim frequently to keep plants compact and full. If your plant looks leggy, cut it back and use the leaves you cut away to season that evening's dinner.

Mexican oregano (*Poliomintha longiflora*) is most often thought of as an herb, and the plant makes a nice shrub that can get 5 feet tall. It has pretty little pinky-lavender blooms that flower from spring to fall and give color as well as flavor to the garden. The foliage is light green, and that is the part you use to flavor your pizza, chili, or any other dish that calls for oregano. The flowers can be added to salads for color and fun. Although the plant tolerates some shade, it prefers full sun. Drought-tolerant and partial to alkaline soil, it is a tough plant that looks great.

Another contender in the not-really-oregano sweepstakes is also called Mexican oregano (*Lippia graveolens*). This herb is native to Mexico, Guatemala, and parts of South America. It is a shrubby bush that grows up to 5 feet tall and wide and has dark green, highly fragrant foliage. Tiny starry-white flowers complement the small leaves. This plant is difficult to find in most areas of the United States, but it is said to have a sweet and intense flavor that works great in recipes.

✸ *Cover up with it.* Use Russian, Greek, Syrian, and other low-growing oreganos as great ground covers. They require little care, are drought-tolerant, don't need good rich soil, and will spread easily to form a luscious green mat. When you step on the plants you will think you have wandered into a delightful pizza parlor! For variety, there are several variegated oreganos that will give a bright gold look to the garden.

✸ *Border with it.* Use the upright Mexican oregano (*Poliomentha longiflora*) as a shrubby plant in your perennial border. Its bright pink flowers will bloom all season and provide edible flowers and delightful flavors, and it also makes a very good landscape plant that blends well with natives and other herbs. This shrub can grow to around 5 feet tall and dies down in the winter only to come back in early spring to bloom again and again.

✸ *Attract with it.* Butterflies and bees love oregano flowers. Keep them happy with different types to offer different blooms.

✸ *Eat it.* Most oreganos are perennial and evergreen in warm gardens, so there is no reason not to use fresh herbs year-round. Remember, fresh is *always* better than dried or frozen. Taste different oreganos to find out which ones you like best. There is a wide range of scents and flavors in this big category. Some are too strong, some are way too weak. Shop around the nursery and sniff the leaves to see which ones meet your criteria.

Oregano is a wonderful companion herb to tomatoes—hence its frequent use in Italian cooking. A sprinkling on fresh sliced tomatoes is delicious. Cooked in sauce, it is divine. You can make a nice bouquet garni to add flavor to stews and soups by tying together stems of oregano, thyme, parsley, and a few bay leaves. Remove the bundle before serving.

✿ *Baste with it.* Tie stems together to form a basting brush. Add minced garlic to a little oil for your baste. Use the oregano brush to baste chicken, fish, or steak and potatoes on the grill.

✿ *Make vinegar with it.* Pack oregano leaves and flowers into a jar or bottle and fill with vinegar. Oregano also combines nicely with other Mediterranean herbs like rosemary and garlic. Use the vinegar to flavor salad dressings, cooked veggies, and meats, stews, and fish.

✿ *Make an herb wreath.* The close clusters of leaves on oregano plants make a great base for herbal wreaths. Fresh or dried, the leaves can cover a wreath form, and the flowers make good accents along with other herb blossoms.

✿ *Soothe with it.* Adding an infusion of oregano to bath water helps some people relax, and chewing on a leaf of oregano may give temporary relief for toothache. Oregano is also said to help aid digestion.

Victor Z. Martin
2007

Parsley *Petroselinum sativum*

☀ *Learn about it.* Parsley was cultivated as early as the third century B.C. The Romans used it as a garnish and flavoring and decorated their tables and floors with it to absorb unpleasant odors. The Greeks tied it to their horses before battles to make them impervious to weapons. Medieval Europeans believed that if you spoke your enemy's name while plucking a sprig of parsley, your enemy would drop down dead. Parsley came to the United States with the early settlers, and it continued to grow widely throughout the country as a culinary herb. We don't use it much to kill enemies any more.

Of all the culinary herbs, parsley is probably the widest known, and probably it is best known as that green, curly thing that restaurants put on your plate. The tradition of putting a sprig on the plate has good reason behind it. The chlorophyll in parsley will help freshen your breath if you chew it after you finish the other food. It's too bad most people just ignore it.

☀ *Grow it.* Parsley is a biennial plant. It produces a nice clump of leaves in the first year of growth and flowers in the second year. The flowers are very attractive to beneficial insects, and, for that reason alone, it deserves a place in the garden. It also makes a lovely border or container plant because it is mannerly and will maintain its compact shape. It prefers cool weather and is more likely to be done in by heat than by cold. In warm climates, plant it in the fall of the year and give it some shelter from afternoon sun and a good mulch in the summer. Once the flowers begin to appear, the plant will die. You can postpone the inevitable by pinching off the flower stalks as they appear. You can also plant a new plant or two every year so you always have some one-year-olds as well as two-year-olds in the garden. Plant in good garden soil and water when it is dry. Pests are rarely a problem.

There are two basic types of parsley: curly leaf and flat leaf. Curly leaf was all we knew for years, but now chefs are telling us that only flat leaf will do. Judge for yourself which one you like better. The curly type is most commonly used as a garnish, while the flat is chopped up in recipes. There is no reason you can't grow both in your garden.

✦ *Give it friends.* Parsley is an excellent companion plant for many other plants. Plant it or sprinkle its leaves among tomato and asparagus plants to encourage growth. Planted beneath or next to roses, parsley will increase the fragrance of the roses and improve their general health. Make an infusion of parsley and spray it on the garden to ward off asparagus beetles.

✦ *Attract with it.* Hoverflies, beneficial wasps, and other predatory insects love parsley flowers. Although they signal the end of that plant, the flowers do have their value. The flowers also attract the swallowtail butterfly. They will lay eggs on the plant and the brightly colored larvae will gobble it up. You can easily move the caterpillars to a less-desirable plant or sacrifice one or two parsley plants for their lunch. These are the same butterflies that love dill and fennel.

✦ *Eat it.* Parsley is an almost universal herb. It blends well with most other flavors and adds a mildly spicy taste of its own. You can snip it into sauces, butters, dressings, or just about any other dish. It is almost always an ingredient in bouquet garni, and who hasn't heard of parsley-sage-rosemary-and-thyme? Parsley is good alone and combines wonderfully with other herbs.

Combine parsley with butter to spread on biscuits, rolls, corn muffins, and broiled meat. Add garlic to that parsley butter and toss with hot pasta, spread on Italian or French bread, or put a dollop on fresh steamed vegetables. Chop parsley and add to salads. Or, add parsley to other herbs when you are making pesto. It will make the other herbs go farther and give the resulting sauce a nice, slightly different flavor.

Whisk into salad dressings and sauces. Add plenty to your holiday stuffing. It has an affinity for most foods, including poultry.

Poultry Seasoning: Mix together 2 cups dried parsley, 1 cup chopped dried sage, ½ cup dried crushed rosemary, ½ cup dried crushed oregano, ½ teaspoon ground ginger, 3 tablespoons salt, 1 teaspoon pepper, 2 teaspoons onion powder. Pour into airtight containers. Shake well before using.

☀ *Stay healthy with it.* Parsley is rich in vitamins, minerals, and antiseptic chlorophyll. It is high in vitamins A and C and contains iron, iodine, and copper. Parsley is sometimes chewed to freshen breath, and a poultice of chopped leaves can be made into an antiseptic dressing for sprains, wounds, and bug bites. An infusion may make a soothing eyebath for someone suffering from tired or strained eyes, and parsley is also said to increase milk in nursing mothers.

CAUTION: Buy your parsley from a nursery, and don't try to find it in the wild. Fool's parsley, a wild plant that looks and smells like parsley, is poisonous and not something you want in your garden or kitchen.

Roses *Rosa* spp.

Victor Z Minton 2000

⭐ *Learn about it.*
There are books and books written about roses. Roses appear frequently in poetry and literature ("A rose is a rose is a rose," "a rose by any other name would smell as sweet," "Moses supposes his toeses are roses"). But, not everyone knows that roses are also herbs.

Roses have been recognized through the ages for their scent and beauty. They seem to have sprouted through-out the northern hemisphere—one type in China and another in Europe—but only when the two types got together did we get the lovely, everblooming varieties we know today. There is fossil evidence of roses dating back 35 million years—now that is a lot of roses!

In the Roman Empire, rose petals were used as confetti at celebrations, in medicines, and as a source of perfume. Large public rose gardens grew south of Rome. During the fifteenth century in England, roses were adopted as symbols of warring factions in the War of the Roses—white roses for the Yorks and red roses for the Lancasters. In the seventeenth century, roses were highly prized in France, so much so that they were bartered for goods and services. In the 1800s, Napoleon's wife Josephine established a rose garden at Chateau de Malmaison that claimed to have one of each variety of rose grown in the world at that time. It was in this garden that the famed artist Redouté did his wonderful botanical paintings.

Late in the eighteenth century, roses from China were introduced into Europe and thus began a frenzy of hybridization. The Chinese roses offered the ability to bloom repeatedly, and rose growers were thrilled. Almost all the roses we know today are the result of breeding between Chinese and European roses.

✤ *Grow it.* Roses are large or small shrubs, moderate to vigorous climbers, and appear in numerous colors, scents, and shapes. Antique roses are enjoying a resurgence of popularity. These old roses are easy to grow, resistant to most diseases, and require much less care than hybrid tea roses. They also are more attractive plants in the garden. On the other hand, hybrid tea roses produce beautiful flowers and sometimes result in more fragrance and better, more nutritious rose hips.

Roses need at least six hours of sun a day. They need good air circulation and they need good, organically-rich soil. That said, there are a lot of old roses growing without anyone's attention or care and doing just fine. The most important element seems to be sun. Rose plants will sometimes grow in the shade, but those plants rarely bloom, and who wants roses without the flowers?

Roses grown on their own roots rather than grafted onto root-stock are healthier and more tolerant of high heat and humidity. You can easily recognize grafted plants because there is a big knot at the bottom of the plant near the ground. This is where the two plants were joined together. Own-root roses just send up canes from the ground. Container grown plants should be put in the ground in the fall so their roots have time to establish themselves before the spring bloom season begins.

Don't believe those people who say roses need a lot of care. Choose the right roses and they need almost no care at all. Once established, they can be drought-tolerant. A good old rose will shake off almost any disease. The trick is finding roses that do well in your climate and conditions. Look around your neighborhood and see which roses you like and find out what they are. There is no reason on earth you cannot grow roses organically.

✸   *Sniff it.* Of course, in addition to their beauty, roses are famous for their smell. Although some roses have no smell at all, many have scents that can cause a grown woman to weep with joy. Roses are the favorite cut flower of almost everyone, so while you have them growing outdoors, enjoy them indoors as well. Even if you have to cut a new batch every day, it is worth the effort to have the wonderful smells and colors in the house.

✸   *Eat it.* Rose petals are edible, but really, they aren't the tastiest food in the world. They are, however, dramatic and showy, so if you want to impress a guest, by all means toss the petals in your salad, pie, vinegar, or whatever. Remove the white heel at the base of the petals before serving. You might try pickling some rosebuds if you have a large supply. You can also crystallize rose petals and use them to decorate cakes and other fancy foods. I even found a recipe for rose petal sandwiches on the Internet, but it involved a lot of other stuff that actually tasted good, so why cover up nice rose petals with slices of bread?

Rose hips, the round seed case that forms when the petals fall off, are often used to make teas, wine, syrup, and jam. Rose hips contain vitamins B, E, K, and are particularly high in vitamin C. They are tastier when combined with other herbs to make tea. Rose hips and lemon balm are a good combination.

✸   *Dry it.* Rose buds are easily dried by hanging them upside-down in a shady spot where there is good air circulation. Choose the buds when they are tight before they begin to open. Those dried flowers can be used in arrangements, bouquets, as decorations in all sorts of ways. You can also dry petals by removing them from the stem, spreading them out on a non-porous surface or screen and letting them dry naturally. Most roses will keep their scent and color once they are dried. Pick the petals when they are fully mature but before they begin to darken around the edges.

Rose Potpourri: Mix together 3 cups dried rose petals and buds, 1 cup dried lemon verbena, 2 cups dried lavender, 1 cup dried calendula petals, 1 tablespoon cinnamon, 1 tablespoon ground allspice, and ½ cup powdered orris root. If you want more scent as time goes by and the original scent fades, you can sprinkle with a few drops of essential oil in the flavor you prefer.

✸ *Sniff it some more.* Roses have been used for perfumes for centuries. You can make your own cologne from your own roses and have a signature scent that combines your favorites.

Rose Petal Cologne: Combine 2 cups strongly scented rose petals, 1 cup dried mint, 2 cups distilled water, and 1 cup vodka. Cover and leave for several days in a spot out of direct light. Strain and use as cologne. If the scent isn't strong enough, you can add a few drops of essential oil.

✸ *Craft with it.* Dried roses and rosebuds and even rose hips are great additions to many decorative crafts. Add them to wreaths to add color and scent. And, if you really have time to spend, make your own rosary. The name of the beads treasured by Catholics around the world comes from the original practice of making the beads from rose petals. The roses were cooked until they were a thick paste, formed into balls, pierced, and strung. The result is a fragrant and impressive craft. Even if you are not Catholic, you can use them as "worry beads" and enjoy the nice rose scent they leave on your hands.

✸ *Soothe with it.* Rosewater has been a component in cosmetic products for many years, and not just because it smells good. Rosewater and glycerin is a famous old skin lotion, and rosewater all by itself is believed to be a good antiseptic tonic to soothe dry, inflamed, mature, or sensitive skin. Some people splash it on their eyes to relax and help relieve conjunctivitis.

One popular method for creating rosewater is to gather 2 cups fresh, fragrant (preferably red) rose petals and place them in a non-reactive pan and cover with rain water, spring water, or distilled water. The mixture is brought almost to a boil, then removed from heat and allowed to cool. Strained and refrigerated, it will stay fresh for several days. Red roses will make a pale pink water. Other colors will produce a yellowish-brown liquid.

✸ *Get hooked on it.* Once you start growing roses, you will want to grow more and more. There are so many choices of color, flower form, plant size, scent, and more that you will want a new plant every time you see one you don't already have. It is a harmless addiction. Give in!

Rosemary *Rosmarinus officinalis*

✦ *Learn about it.* Rosemary is an ancient herb that grew wild in the Mediterranean area and was used by ancient Romans and Greeks as a fragrance and as a medicinal and magical herb. It was one herb easily available to the poor since it grew wild and was widely used for all sorts of purposes. Putting it under the bed or pillow was said to ensure a good night's sleep and pleasant dreams. It was also widely known as an herb that enhances memory—William Shakespeare is famous for so many things, including saying that rosemary is for remembrance: "There's rosemary for you, that's for remembrance! Pray you, love, remember" (Ophelia in *Hamlet*). And while it really didn't work out too well for Ophelia, modern research is proving that the old belief has some merit. Rosemary does seem to contain properties that increase the memory and stimulate mental health.

As a token of memory, rosemary is often used as part of bridal bouquets and in funeral floral offerings. It was burned in shrines and homes in Greece to chase away evil spirits and cleanse the space. A necklace or garland of rosemary was said to keep the wearer youthful. Of course, it was also said to attract elves, so you might want to keep that in mind. What is the good of being forever young if you are surrounded by pesky elves?

Another nice belief was that where rosemary grew, the woman ruled.

❋ *Grow it.* Rosemary does very well in warm climate gardens. It likes heat, sun, and rocky soil. Excellent drainage is a must. If you grow your rosemary in a container, add large-grained sand or gravel to your rich potting soil to make sure the drainage is very good. Choose a spot with a lot of sun and good air circulation. This is particularly important in humid areas where mildew can become a problem.

In cold climates, you can grow rosemary in a container and bring it inside to a sunny spot in the winter.

Whether you grow a huge hedge of upright rosemary, cover the side of a sunny hill with prostrate rosemary, or have a little pot sitting on the back porch, no home should be without rosemary.

Rosemary demands very little care. It takes occasional watering if the weather is dry, a good water-soluble organic fertilizer every now and then during the growing season, and a gardener to enjoy its fragrance and beauty.

There are many varieties of rosemary available at your local nursery. Some have pink flowers; some have blue flowers. Some have wide leaves; some have very narrow leaves. The subtle differences in scent and flavor make it fun to try new varieties. All are easy to grow and an essential part of any garden and kitchen.

❋ *Create a topiary.* Rosemary will easily grow into a variety of shapes—wreaths, single or double balls, or cone shapes. Simply plant and train as the plant grows.

❋ *Cook with it.* Rosemary's piney flavor has an affinity for foods rich in fat, such as roast meats, poultry, and fish, or with bland foods, such as potatoes or legumes. It is a good addition to soups and stews. Use whole pieces and remove them before serving.

Rosemary is a strong herb, so use small amounts of leaves wisely, but use it often. Its flavor adds zest to bland foods like potatoes and depth to meats like chicken, beef, and lamb. Combine it with other herbs to make a perfect blend of taste to flavor almost anything.

You can also barbeque with it. Cut branches of the plant and toss them on the coals in your barbeque to give the meat a delightful flavor. Use stripped branches as skewers to thread your favorite meats and veggies on before cooking. The flavor will steep in from the inside and infuse your food with wonderful taste.

★ *Have a cookie.* Rosemary Treats: Combine ¼ cup packed light brown sugar, 2 eggs, beaten, and ½ tsp vanilla. Mix well. Sift together 1 cup all-purpose flour, 1 tsp baking powder, and ½ tsp salt. Gradually add to egg mixture. Sprinkle with 1 tablespoon fresh rosemary leaves, chopped. Fold in 1 cup chopped pecans, 4 ounces white raisins, and 4 ounces mixed candied cherries and pineapple pieces. Spread evenly into a greased and floured 8-inch square pan. Bake at 375° for 30 minutes. Remove from pan and cool before slicing.

★ *Drink it.* On a hot day, nothing is better than Rosemary Fizz: Simmer 2 tablespoons crushed rosemary, 3 tablespoons sugar, and ½ cup water with a pinch of salt for 2 minutes. Cool and strain. Combine with ½ cup lime juice, 8 ounce apricot nectar, and 1 quart ginger ale. Serve over ice and garnish with rosemary and lime slices.

★ *Deter with it.* Protect your fine linens and winter woolies. Rosemary placed in among your linens will protect them from insect pests. Put it in a sachet and its scent will please you and drive pests away. Hang some branches in your closet to serve the same purpose there.

★ *Decorate with it.* Rosemary is a perfect holiday decoration. Use it in wreaths, garlands, bouquets, and centerpieces. Because it is evergreen, it is ready to bring indoors to decorate. You can even find or grow rosemary topiaries trimmed to Christmas tree shapes that are ready for decoration.

★ *Freshen with it.* Tie a handful of branches together and hang in the closet to make it smell good and discourage moths. A bouquet of rosemary branches will freshen the air in any room. Run your hand over the leaves periodically to release the essential oils.

★ *Clean house with it.* Combine rosemary with vinegar and use the mixture to clean your kitchen and bathroom. Add vinegar to the mop water or to water to clean the windows. It will deodorize and sanitize all hard surfaces except wood and leave your room sparkling without exposing you to harmful chemicals.

Rosemary Disinfectant: Simmer a handful of leaves and small stems for 30 minutes in water to cover them. The less water the more disinfecting power. Strain and use to clean sinks and bathrooms or to give a fresh scent to rooms by spraying into the air. Add dishwashing liquid to get rid of grease on surfaces. Store the mixture in the refrigerator for up to a week.

✸ *Relax with it.* If you have dark hair, a rinse with an infusion of rosemary after shampooing will bring out the highlights and make your hair smell wonderful. It is also said to treat greasy hair and dandruff and even encourage hair growth. A good splash of a strong rosemary infusion in the bath is relaxing and refreshing.

✸ *Soothe with it.* Rosemary tea, made by steeping the leaves in boiling water for about five minutes, has been used for many purposes. It is said to be good for promoting memory and mental acuity. Sipping the tea on a winter day may sooth harried nerves, make a sore throat feel better, and help stave off a cold or the flu.

Rue *Ruta graveolens*

Victor Z. Martin
2006

✸ *Learn about it.* Rue is one of the oldest garden plants, having been cultivated since the sixteenth century. It is native to southern Europe and was believed to have healing and magical powers. Common names were herb of grace, herbygrass, rutae herba, and vinruta.

It was believed to have the power to counteract witchcraft and to enhance psychic abilities. It also was used throughout the world as a medicinal herb for many centuries, but most authorities no longer recommend it for internal use.

✸ *Grow it.* Rue makes a lovely landscape plant. Its flowers are easily dried, and they add a light airy effect to dried arrangements. In the garden, it makes a beautiful green clumping plant with the flowers waving above the foliage. It is a hardy evergreen plant that will grow in very poor soil. The bluish green leaves are attractive, and the greenish-yellow flowers blossom from spring until fall.

✸ *Don't eat it.* For generations, rue was known as a medicinal herb. Today scientists say the ingredients are too strong and too risky for home use.

CAUTION: Although you can find recipes for remedies on the Internet and in old herbal books, it is strongly advised that this herb *not* be taken internally.

★ *Deter with it.* One of rue's traditional uses is to repel insects and other pests. It is a good companion plant for roses, berries, and other vegetables because it helps to deter Japanese beetles. In ancient days, it was used to repel fleas and other biting insects. According to Maude Grieve in *A Modern Herbal,* "Rue has been regarded from the earliest times as successful in warding off contagion and preventing the attacks of fleas and other noxious insects. It was the custom for judges sitting at assizes to have sprigs of rue placed on the bench of the dock against the pestilential infection brought into court from gaol (jail) by the prisoner, and the bouquet still presented in some districts to judges at the assizes was originally a bunch of aromatic herbs, given to him for the purpose of warding off gaol-fever." I have also heard that, placed on the doorstep, it will keep old boyfriends and bad people away.

CAUTION: Rue contains volatile oils in its leaves that make some people break out. Don't crush the leaves against your skin and don't work in it during the heat of the day or in bright sunlight when the oils are most active.

Sage *Salvia officinalis*

Victor Z. Martin
2007

✺ *Learn about it.* Sage has been grown in Europe since the Middle Ages. It is a native of the Mediterranean area and Asia Minor and has a long history as a medicinal herb. In fact, the Latin name *Salvia* means to save, referring to its healing properties. An ancient proverb says, "No man should die who has sage in his garden." Well, sage may not be that good, but the Greeks used it to treat consumption, ulcers, and snake bites. The ancient Romans considered it a sacred herb and had elaborate rituals and tools just to pick it. The Chinese were fond of sage as well and would trade three chests of China tea for one chest of sage.

✺ *Grow it.* Garden sage likes to grow in the full sun and in dry soil. It likes limestone soils. Sage is a good garden plant for warm climates. It is drought-tolerant and not attractive to many pests. The light gray-green leaves are a beautiful contrast to the darker green of many garden plants, and in the spring, if you are lucky, a profusion of luscious lavender-pink flowers will bloom and last quite a long time. Even though sage is a perennial herb, in more humid climates it will need replacing about every three years.

It is best to grow sage from cuttings or nursery plants. You can see the leaves on young plants and know what you are getting. Sage seeds are often unreliable.

Prune back the plant after flowering to encourage new growth and get rid of spent flower stalks. Garden sage is happy growing in containers as long as the drainage is good and there is plenty of sun.

Several varieties of sage are available for planting in the garden. Common garden sage comes in purple, gold, variegated, and combinations of colors. Pineapple sage is a tender perennial that will die back in cooler climates. It produces a beautiful red flower and has a nice pineapple scent. Clary sage is a large and beautiful plant that was often used in wine and beer making. It is a biennial and produces a lovely flower stalk. There is also a whole world of ornamental salvias, but those are rarely used as herbs.

✶ *Plant near friends.* Broccoli, cauliflower, rosemary, cabbage, carrots, strawberries, and tomatoes all benefit from being planted near sage.

✶ *Avoid enemies.* Don't plant sage near cucumbers, onions, or rue.

✶ *Eat it.* Sage improves the digestion of foods, and that is one reason it is often used in sausages and other fatty meat dishes. It is best known, however, as an ingredient in holiday dressings or stuffings. Sage is a strongly flavored herb and can easily overpower a dish. When you are cooking with it, start with a small amount and increase gradually until you have the taste you want.

Both the flowers and the leaves of herb varieties are edible. The flowers are attractive in salads and good for making tea, and the leaves are great for cooking and making herb butters and vinegars.

Sage mixes well with cheese as well as meats. Chive-Sage Cheese Log: Grate 8 ounces sharp cheddar cheese and add ½ cup chopped fresh sage and ½ cup chopped chives. You can do this in a food processor. Add 8 ounces cream cheese at room temperature and blend by hand. Roll into a log in plastic wrap and refrigerate until firm. If you have chive or sage blossoms, you can roll the log in them before chilling for a pretty and unusual look. Serve with crisp bread or crackers for a good party dish or hors d'ouevres.

✱   *Attract with it.* Sage attracts bumblebees, butterflies, hummingbirds, and other essential pollinators. The flowers are also attractive to many beneficial predatory insects.

✱   *Deter with it.* Sage planted near cabbage is said to help repel cabbage moths. It also repels moths in the linen closet. A bouquet of leaves hung to dry will keep moths out of the closet, and a sachet in chests will do the same. It also repels other insects that get into cloth.

✱   *Decorate with it.* Sage flowers are beautiful additions to springtime bouquets. The tall spikes of lavender flowers blend well with roses, daisies, and other garden flowers. They are long-lasting and smell nice. The red pineapple sage flowers are lovely in the fall and combine with other fall flowers and foliage.

You can also use dried sage leaves and flowers in wreaths, bouquets, and potpourri.

✱   *Freshen with it.* Sage has long been known as a cleansing herb. Burn it on embers or boil in water to disinfect a room. Sage smoke deodorizes animal and cooking smells. You can burn loose dried sage leaves in a small container. Close off the room you are trying to cleanse and let the smoldering smoke work its magic.

You can make a good air freshener by combining dried sage flowers, rosemary, ground cloves, and baking soda. Crush and sprinkle the mix onto the carpet and leave for an hour or so. Vacuum up the mixture and the room will smell great for a while.

✱   *Soothe with it.* Sage not only is tasty but it also has several strong medicinal characteristics. Sage has natural antibacterial properties, which makes it useful in the preservation of meat and is the reason it is so often included in sausage recipes. It is also the reason that sage is sometimes used to clean the air.

The leaves of sage act as a powerful astringent. Native Americans rubbed the fresh leaves of sage on their teeth as a cleanser. Similarly, canker sores have been treated by chewing the leaves and using them as a poultice. Because sage also slows down the secretions of fluids, a sage tea has been used by some people to slow down excessive sweating (including night sweats), vaginal discharge, and diarrhea. It may also slow milk production, so nursing women should not use it unless they are ready to wean.

Sage tea with honey and lemon, or a gargle of tea and a little apple cider vinegar, are said to ease sore throats and colds.

CAUTION: Culinary use of sage is harmless and tasty, but use of the concentrated amounts in sage tea must be limited to only a week or two. Sage contains a volatile oil, thujone, which may act as a neurotoxin. Prolonged and concentrated use of this chemical can damage your nervous system.

Tansy *Tanacetum vulgare*

☀ *Learn about it.* **Native to Europe, tansy has a long history as a folk medicine. Because of its strong antiseptic properties, it was used in ancient embalming practices. It was also used as a strewing herb in the Middle Ages because of its ability to repel insects. According to liquor historian A. J. Baime, Jack Daniels liked to drink his bourbon with sugar and crushed tansy leaf.**

CAUTION: Tansy contains the chemical thujone, which is also a poisonous component in absinthe, and can be harmful when taken internally.

☀ *Grow it.* The lovely fern-like leaves of the tansy, coupled with the bright yellow button flowers, make it a nice landscape plant. It can become invasive, however, so either put it where it can roam or contain it some way. Easy to grow, it will remain evergreen in Zone 8 at least. It will grow 3–4 feet tall in some spots, but can be kept smaller if grown in a container.

Grow near fruit trees to repel pests and to encourage growth of roses, raspberries, and other fruiting trees and bushes.

✸ *Deter with it.* One of the traditional uses of tansy is to plant it by the door so that it will keep flies away. A clump at doorways is attractive as well as useful. The yellow flowers remain on the plant for a long time, giving it a colorful look. The plant repels ants and fleas as well as flies. Chop and crush the foliage and sprinkle on ant pathways. You can also use it in the house if you have a stubborn ant problem or on spots where the dog or cat are inclined to bring fleas.

Put dried sprigs of tansy under rugs to keep away bugs. Mice are also said to run from dried leaves sprinkled in their path.

Native Americans crushed the leaves and rubbed them on their skin to keep mosquitoes and other biting insects away. The dried root of tansy is a strong insect-repellant. When your clump gets out of control, take some of the root, dry and crush it, and use it to repel pest insects inside and out.

✸ *Cut it.* Both leaves and flowers make a nice addition to any cut flower arrangement. The leaves are airy and are good filler and background plant material for brightly colored flowers. The yellow flowers add texture and color to any bouquet.

✸ *Dry it.* The yellow button-like flowers of the Tansy plant dry easily and are favorites to add to dried arrangements, wreaths, and potpourris. They are long-lasting and add a bright note to any dried craft.

✸ *Dye with it.* Yellow dye from the flowers and green dye from the roots can be used in any project that uses natural dyes.

Thyme *Thymus vulgaris*

Victor Z. Martin
2007

☀ *Learn about it.* Thyme is another Mediterranean herb that has become essential in world-wide cuisine. It grows wild in the region and has been used since ancient times. Called the "scent of the Mediterranean," thyme is fragrant and attractive. Roman soldiers bathed in thyme water for vigor and courage in battle. The Greeks also believed it had magical powers. Because of its powerful antiseptic and preservative components, it was part of the embalming process perfected by ancient Egyptians. This association with death extended into subsequent years, and thyme branches were often tossed onto the coffin of a departed loved one to ensure safe passage into the next world. In later centuries, thyme spread throughout Europe and on to Britain, where it grew wild on the wide, abandoned moors. The association of thyme with courage also persisted, and the herb was used as a symbol of the bravery of those who plotted the French Revolution.

☀ *Grow it.* There are many varieties of thyme from which to choose. The plants cross-pollinate easily, so natural hybrids are always popping up to add to the long list of hybrids that plant hybridizers develop. There are three main groups of thyme: the upright varieties that grow up to

18 inches tall, the creeping varieties that are about 6 inches tall, and the very flat types that grow only 1–2 inches tall. The upright varieties are the ones most often used for cooking. The other varieties are attractive garden plants with great looking leaves and flowers and a nice, clean scent. French, English, lemon, and common thyme are the most widely available of the upright varieties.

Thyme insists on perfect drainage. You can kill thyme quicker with soggy soil than any other way. It also likes heat, sun, and rocky soil. Many people plant creeping and very low-growing thymes between paving stones and as ground cover. It can take a certain amount of foot traffic and looks and smells great when growing among flat stones. You can use different shades and forms together to give a textured look to your walkway. All of the thymes look good and natural when planted in rocky areas since that is their natural habitat.

Thyme also grows well in containers if you use a loose soil mix that will drain well. The trailing and low-growing types look great combined with more upright plants in a large container. Just be sure that all the plants in the pot need the same amount of water—not much in the case of thyme.

The stems of thyme plants tend to become woody after a little while, so trim the plants often to keep new growth appearing. Snip back often because a rare, severe pruning may kill your plant. Once established, thyme is virtually carefree. It requires little water, little fertilization, and no pest control.

In humid climates, you may have to replace your plants every few years. Thyme just hates all that moisture!

✶ *Eat it.* Thyme is an essential culinary herb in most cuisines. Combined with bay and parsley it makes up the classic bouquet garni that is used in soups, stews, and other dishes. Although the leaves are small, the taste of thyme is large, so use sparingly to begin with. Find out how much you and your family like before tossing in handfuls!

To use thyme, strip the small leaves from the stems. All but the youngest green stems are too woody to use in cooking.

Lemon thyme, like other lemon herbs, has an affinity for fish and enhances the flavor of baked or broiled fish dishes or fish sauces. It also makes a refreshing hot or cold tea.

Thyme Cheese Roll: Combine 8 ounces softened cream cheese, 1 tablespoon chopped thyme, 1 tablespoon chopped parsley, ½ teaspoon minced garlic. Roll into a log and refrigerate. Serve with toast or crackers for a quick and easy snack. You can vary the recipe by changing up the herbs. Use basil instead of parsley or add toasted nuts. Experiment and use your imagination.

✺ *Attract with it.* Bees love thyme flowers. They will be happy to browse among the flowers for hours, and we do want those bees in our gardens! In addition, the blossoms of thyme make great honey. Other beneficial insects are also attracted to the tiny blooms.

✺ *Deter with it.* Planted in the vegetable garden, thyme is said to help deter cabbage worms.

✺ *Clean with it.* Because of its antiseptic powers, thyme makes a good household cleaner. Use a decoction of the leaves for cleaning bathrooms and kitchens. The scent it leaves behind will be fresh and pleasant.

✺ *Get pretty with it.* Using thyme in a facial steam will open the pores and freshen your complexion as it increases circulation. Adding it to bath water will have the same effect all over your body.

✺ *Soothe with it.* Like all ancient herbs thought to contain mystical powers (concoctions of thyme were said to help you see the fairies), thyme was credited with having healing powers as well. It does contain powerful components that act as an antiseptic and aid digestion. It helps break down fatty foods and is said also to give relief for hangovers. Tea with honey is said to be good for coughs, colds, and sore throats. The tea has also been used as a gargle and mouthwash for sore throats and gums.

For cold and flu, a common treatment is to add 1 grated onion and 2 tablespoons thyme leaves to 2 cups boiling water, steep for 30 minutes, strain, and add lemon juice. The onion contains compounds that help relax bronchial muscles and prevent spasms. The thyme contains antiseptic and antibacterial properties.

Vetiver Grass *Vetiveria zizanioides*

✲ *Learn about it.* Vetiver grass, a member of the same part of the grass family as maize, sorghum, sugar cane, and lemon grass, is an ancient plant that has grown around the world to great benefit for centuries. Like many plants, however, vetiver has fallen out of fashion and become forgotten or unknown through the years.

A native of India, vetiver has a long history. The name comes from "vetiver," a Tamil word meaning "root that is dug up." The Latin name *zizanioides* was given by Carl Linnaeus in 1771 and means "by the riverside." As you would guess, the native habitat of this grass is in low, damp sites such as swamps and bogs.

✲ *Grow it.* The above-ground plant looks much like pampas grass or lemon grass. It is a big, coarse, clumping grass that can grow to be very tall. It provides a considerable amount of biomass that can be used for mulching or composting. In many areas of the world, the grass is used for thatching roofs.

The crown of the plant is adaptable to rising soil levels. As the sediment builds up around the plant, the crown grows upward and is not damaged by soil being piled around it. Although vetiver goes dormant in the winter or very dry seasons, its stems and leaves stay stiff and firmly attached to the crown. This means that the plant continues to stop soil movement even though it is not actively growing.

Young plants may dry up in the hot sun before they are well established if they don't receive ample water. Older plants are very drought-tolerant and require no additional water beyond natural rainfall. Once established, the plant is difficult to kill. There are surviving plants in Louisiana that were planted before the Civil War that continue to grow and flourish despite total neglect. Sometimes damping-off fungus is a problem in the young plants; otherwise disease and pests are rarely a problem.

Vetiver is a tropical plant and will not survive cold winters. One authority says that its northern limit is probably Austin, Texas, although given protection, mild winters, and heavy mulching it will grow farther north.

The biggest problem with vetiver grass is finding it. If you can find someone growing the grass, it is easy to divide and propagate. Taking a small slice of the root and growing it in a pot will result in many slips within a short period of time.

✱ *Control erosion with it.* In spite of its natural affinity for damp locations, the grass is now being used on dry hillsides to control erosion. In 1989, Fort Polk in Louisiana was having a problem with erosion. Three scenic streams came together on the base, but tanks and other military equipment were ripping up the land and causing soil and silt to fill up the natural waterways. The local U.S. Soil Conservation Service agent brought in some vetiver plants and planted them in the bare slopes above the dams that held runoff water.

In spite of the very acidic, rocky, and hardly fertile soil, the slips of grass began to grow. In eight weeks, some were almost 6½ feet tall, and in ten weeks they had grown together into hedges. Sediment began to build up behind the hedges and the water that went down the streams into the catch ponds became clear.

It soon became evident that vetiver was acting as much more than an erosion trap: it was a "nurse plant" that was protecting other species and thereby giving these devastated watersheds a chance to heal themselves. Native grasses, wildflowers, shrubs, trees, and vines came crowding in behind the hedges and grew to revegetate the site.

Madelene Hill has been growing vetiver in her herb garden at Festival Hill in Round Top, Texas, for the past several years. It serves as a border plant on a steep raised bed which previously had washed away during heavy rains.

John Riley at the Kika de la Garza Plant Materials Center in Kingsville, Texas, says they evaluated the grass as a possible plant to be used in rangeland and wetlands restoration, specifically in gully erosion control. They found it to be non-invasive and very effective in filtering and controlling runoff.

Circle C, a large development near Austin, Texas, has used vetiver in landscaping to control erosion in its environmentally sensitive Hill Country location.

✸ *Make perfume with it.* The roots of the plant have been used for centuries as a source of essential oil that makes a wonderful perfume. It is also used for scenting soaps.

✸ *Root for it.* It is the root of the plant that makes it valuable—whether for perfume or erosion control. Vetiver produces a massive root system that grows straight down rather than out from the plant. It creates a sort of curtain beneath the soil, trapping sediment and slowing down the movement of water. Because the grass grows down instead of outward, it does not become invasive. The plants never form seeds, another advantage that keeps it under control.

Other Good Things to Do with My Herbs

The list of things to do with herbs is almost unlimited. They are the most versatile of plants, yet one of the best things to do with them is just to plant and enjoy them. Herbs make wonderful landscape plants that should not be confined to "herb gardens." Many common trees are listed in classic herbal books as useful plants: sycamore, elm, oak, and pine all have parts that have been used to make medicine or other products. The bark of the willow tree contains the substance from which aspirin is derived. Gingko and vitex trees have long and continued use as medicinal plants.

Shrubs such as bay laurel, roses, and rosemary are wonderful land-scaping plants that can serve as foundation planting or as hedges. Vines such as passion vine, hop, and black pepper can climb and trail through your garden. Perennials and annuals will provide color, texture, scent, and interest to any garden. They can be used as groundcovers or specimen plants, in containers on the patio or next to the curb in the hottest spot in the yard.

For too long, people have thought of herbs as tender, small, and specialized. They are wildly versatile plants that reward the gardener with a multitude of benefits with minimal effort. One of the best things about herbs is that most of them make very few demands on their caretakers. Put them in the ground, get them established with a little water, and they are off and growing.

The next time you are looking for a plant to fill a spot in the garden, consider herbs. They always serve a multitude of purposes—multi-tasking is an herbal skill! They look good, smell good, taste good, or at least keep the bugs away. I can't think of a single herb that just sits there and does nothing, which is more than I can say for lawn grass, for instance.

On the other hand, don't feel honor-bound to do something with your herbs just because they are willing. It is perfectly fine to just plant and enjoy them in the garden. You do not have to *do* anything! Some gardeners enjoy herbs as "pet plants." When they walk by the rosemary, for example, they give it a pat and enjoy the wonderful smell that is released, something you can't always say about Fido, either.

One of the best things you can do with your herbs is share them. Whether you make them into gifts—bouquets, potpourri, bath or clothing sachets, jelly, or wreaths—or just share cuttings, you are spreading the joy of herbs. Most herbs are easily propagated. Many grow from cuttings or root divisions, and you can pass along your favorites while renewing your plant at the same time.

Herbs have been around a long time, and with any luck, they will be around for a while longer. Teach your children and grandchildren to appreciate this wonderful group of plants and to respect all that the plants have to offer. But, also teach them that herbs are great to experiment with, that they are tough plants that do not need babying, and that they are the answer to a lazy gardener's prayer. In short, herbs are fun. They are not a responsibility, they are an opportunity to express your creativity in the kitchen or the craft room or to express your total lack of interest in doing anything but sitting on the porch and smelling the breeze as it blows through the artemisia.

Thanks

Real herbalists are generous and passionate people. They share their knowledge, information, and time to teach others about the plants they love. This book would not have been possible without those people. Cathy Slaughter has shared her time and wisdom through many years to teach me about herbs. Ellen Zimmerman, Madelene Hill, Gwen Barclay, and many others have always been generous with information. I am grateful for all the help that has come down through the centuries, through many books, through the Internet, and especially from the mouths of women who know of what they speak.

Thanks also go to my family for their help, especially to Jenny Turner, who proofread and contributed her perspective; to Sarah Chance, who has proofread for me for years; and to Bob Helberg, who consistently offers good advice, always beginning with "put the last paragraph first." They formed a small but effective cheering squad that kept encouraging and supporting me through the process.

Of course, any mistakes that remain are mine alone.

Index

meetin' seed, 47, 52
Melissa officinalis, 82
Mentha spp., 92
Mexican mint marigold, 88
Mexican oregano, 99
migraine, 55
mint, 3, 4, 23, 65. 87. 92
mint lemonade recipe, 65
mint julep recipe, 94
mint relish recipe, 94
mint tea recipe, 94
Monarda didyma, 17
mosquito chasing oil recipe, 27
mosquito spritz recipe, 27
mugwort, 7
mullein, 96

Nepeta cataria, 26
nervousness, 31, 81, 112

Ocymum basilicum, 10
oregano, 99
Origanum spp., 99
Oswego tea, 18

paper making, 66
parsley, 102, 122
Pelagonium spp., 63
pennyroyal, 90
peppermint, 92
pesto recipe, 11
pest repellant, 8, 12, 15, 27, 39, 48, 54,
    55, 61, 81, 83, 85, 91, 95, 103, 111,
    114, 119, 120, 123
Petroslinum sativum, 102
pigweed, 50

pot marigold, 24
potpourri, 2, 15, 18, 55, 65, 81, 83, 91, 107
poultice, 3, 43, 46
poultry seasoning recipe, 104

refried bean recipe, 51
ristras, 36
roasted garlic recipe, 60
rocambole, 59
Rosa spp., 105
rose, 105, 122
rose petal cologne, 108
rose water recipe, 66, 108
Rosmarinus officinalis, 109
rosemary, 2, 27, 65, 101, 104, 109, 111,
    117, 122
rosemary disinfectant, 111
rosemary fizz recipe, 111
rosemary treats recipe, 111
rue, 113
Ruta graveolens, 113

saffron, 25
sage, 104, 115
salad burnet, 22
salad burnet butter, 23
salad burnet dressing, 23
salad burnet vinegar, 23
Salvia officinalis, 115
Sanguisorba minor, 22
scented geranium, 63
scented geranium cake, 65
scented geranium lemonade recipe, 65
Scoville units, 33
silver king, 7
silver queen, 7

ISBN-13: 978-1-60344-092-9
ISBN-10: 1-60344-092-5